Maxwell Tylden Masters

Plant Life on the Farm

Maxwell Tylden Masters

Plant Life on the Farm

ISBN/EAN: 9783337095161

Printed in Europe, USA, Canada, Australia, Japan

Cover: Foto ©Lupo / pixelio.de

More available books at **www.hansebooks.com**

PLANT LIFE ON THE FARM.

BY
MAXWELL T. MASTERS, M.D., F.R.S.

NEW YORK:
ORANGE JUDD COMPANY,
751 BROADWAY.
1885.

Entered, according to Act of Congress, in the year 1884, by the
ORANGE JUDD COMPANY,
In the Office of the Librarian of Congress, at Washington.

PREFACE.

Rightly to understand what work is done by living plants, and how it is effected, not only requires a student to be a botanist in the ordinary sense of the word, but necessitates that he should also have a comprehensive knowledge of physics and of chemistry.

In few individuals can such an extensive knowledge now-a-days be expected. The practical cultivator especially, harrassed by the daily cares of his occupation, is not able to master the endless details of these sciences; and yet experience shows the increasing necessity for furnishing him with new tools and new weapons to enable him to utilize the resources of Nature, and to contend against adverse circumstances. Such tools, such weapons are furnished by the armory of science. It is the object of this Handbook to point out the nature of these resources, and suggest the methods of utilizing them. Something will be gained if only a right appreciation of what cannot be done is obtained, as thereby labor on a sterile soil will be avoided, to be applied with more reasonable hope of success elsewhere.

In the following pages an attempt has, therefore, been made to supply a sketch, necessarily in faintest outline, of the physiology or life-history of plants; of the way in which they are affected by the circumstances under which they exist, and of the manner in which they in their turn react upon other living beings and upon natural forces. Of necessity, there has been a little overlapping in the case of some of the subjects treated of in the companion volume, "The Chemistry of the Farm," by Mr. Warington; but as the matters are looked at from a different stand-point, and as no pretence is here made to impart special chemical knowledge, it is hoped that Mr. Warington and the reader also will forgive any slight incursions into a territory which the writer has no claim to enter except upon sufferance.

Structural botany, whether dealing with the outer conformation or the internal organization of plants, is only incidentally treated of in these pages; the classification of plants is also passed over without notice, as not coming within the scope of this Handbook.

Detailed text-books of Botany, or of Vegetable Physiology, expressly adapted to the requirements of agriculturists do not exist, but there are many works from which a comprehensive general idea of the present state of knowledge of these subjects may be obtained.

In the compilation of the following pages the writer has availed himself of Van Tieghem's "Traité de Botanique," the French translation of Sachs' "Physiologie Végétale" by Micheli, and Dehérain's "Cours de Chimie Agricole," etc. The works and memoirs of Darwin have, of course, been laid under contribution, as well as numerous scattered papers by various authors. More especially the writer has to acknowledge his obligations to the voluminous records of the noble series of cultural experiments carried out at Rothamsted for so many years by Sir J. B. Lawes and Dr. Gilbert. The "Memorandum Sheet" published by these experimenters supplies annually a condensed summary of the results of their experiments, and is a document that should be carefully studied with due reference to its professed object, by all who have the advancement of agricultural knowledge at heart.

M. T. M.

CONTENTS.

CHAP.	PAGE.
I.—PLANT NUTRITION: THE WORK AND THE MATERIALS	7– 21
II.—NUTRITION.—THE MACHINERY	22– 44
III.—GROWTH	44– 55
IV.—SENSITIVENESS	56– 70
V.—DEVELOPMENT	71– 81
VI.—MULTIPLICATION	81– 89
VII.—THE BATTLE OF LIFE	89–109
VIII.—PRACTICAL INFERENCES	109–124
IX.—DECAY AND DEATH	124–130
INDEX	131–132

PLANT LIFE ON THE FARM.

CHAPTER I.

PLANT-NUTRITION: THE WORK AND THE MATERIALS.

Introductory remarks.—What plants do and how they do it.—Receipts. — Expenditure. — Accumulation. — Transformation. — How plants feed.—Influence of temperature.—Water and the machinery by which it is supplied and distributed.—Protoplasm.—Cells and their contents.—Ingress and movements of water.—The first stage of nutrition.—Diffusion.—Osmosis and the requisite conditions for it. —Saturation.—Varying degrees of, according to the nature of the liquid.—Amount absorbed.—Supply and demand.—Differences of composition of plants grown in the same soil, how explained.— Continuous change.—Nutritive value of water.—Nitrates; agency of Bacteria. — Potash. —Sulphur. — Phosphorus.—Iron.—Lime.— Principles of manuring.—Power of selection.

He who can make two blades of grass grow where only one grew before is universally looked on as a benefactor to his kind. No one will dispute his title to our gratitude; but at the same time it must not be overlooked that the claims of him who can make one grow where none at all existed before, are even greater, because the difficulties to be overcome are more formidable, for where one exists already it is relatively easy to bring about its increase.

In any case, it is clear that, before either problem can be satisfactorily solved, as full a knowledge as possible of all the conditions requisite for the process must be in some way or another obtained. Success in a practical pursuit like agriculture, depends largely on the extent of our knowledge, and still more upon our power of applying it under various circumstances. In the following notes an attempt will be made to supply indications of some among the phenomena of the life of plants of which it seems most desirable that the cultivator should take heed. Some slight knowledge of the general conformation of plants on the part of the reader is assumed, but explanations of the more important points will be given.

A living plant feeds, breathes, grows, developes, multiplies, decays, and ultimately dies. In so doing it receives, it spends, it accumulates, it changes. Some of these processes are always in operation, very generally more than one is going on at the same time, and the action of one is modified by and controlled by that of another. Some circumstances and conditions favor these operations, others hinder them. The practical cultivator has his concern in all these matters, so that it is of no slight moment to him to realize what is the work which a plant does, and how it does it.

How Plants Feed.—The nutritive process has to be entered on the creditor side as a receipt. The plant will indeed feed upon itself for a time, or rather it will feed upon what its predecessor left it as an inheritance for this very purpose, or upon the stores accumulated in the plant itself during the preceding season ; thus, when a seed, or rather the young plant within the seed, begins to grow, it is at first unable to forage for itself, but it depends for its sustenance on the materials laid up for its use during the preceding season by the parent plant. So the bud of a tree awakening into life, and beginning its career as a shoot which is to bear leaves and flowers, derives its first meals from the reserves accumulated the autumn previously in the parent branch. Very generally a little water, supplied from without, is required before the plant can avail itself of these stored-up provisions, but this is not always indispensable. Potatoes begin to sprout in their cellars or pits, as growers know to their cost, before they can have obtained a drop of water from without. In this latter case there is water enough already in the tuber to allow of food being utilized.

Effect of Temperature.—A certain degree of useful heat is, of course, quite indispensable. Practically, no plant will feed when its temperature is reduced as low as the freezing point, and in most cases the heat requires to be considerably greater. Each kind of plant, each individual plant, and indeed each part of a plant, feeds, and performs each item of its life-work, best at a certain temperature, and ceases to work at all when the temperature falls below or rises above a certain point. The particular degree, whether most or least favorable, varies according to the plant, its age, stage of growth and various external circumstances, which we need only mention, as their effects will be readily understood without the necessity of explanation.

It is clear then that a suitable temperature and access of water, either liquid or in the form of vapor, are the first essentials in the feeding process in plants. Practically, and from force of circumstances, the gardener has more control over both temperature and the supply of water than the farmer; nevertheless by drainage, by choice of aspect, site, by shelter, and other means, even the farmer has some power to regulate the temperature and the amount or influence of water to which his crops are subjected.

Water.—Leaving, however, on one side, the temperature, we have to consider the water which is so essential, not only in the feeding processes with which we are now concerned, but with every other action of plant life.

Fortunately there is, in general, no lack of it; the earth and the air contain their shares of this elementary compound in varying proportions and varying modifications as liquid or gaseous. Besides, the plant itself has so much of it that even at the driest condition compatible with life, it still constitutes a very large proportion of the entire weight. Now, it is as a rule when the plant, the seedling, or the bud is at its driest that growth begins, the necessity for food first manifests itself, and the demand for a further supply of water becomes imperative. How is the demand supplied? We have seen that there is no lack of that fluid. How is it to get into the plant? The answer to this question brings us at once to the consideration of the raw material and of the fabric of plants by whose agency alone it is that the water gains entrance to the plant.

Ingress and Movements of Water; Diffusion, Osmosis.—Our first inquiry, then, must be to ascertain how the water, whose presence in sufficient quantity we have assumed, gets from without through the cell-membrane into the protoplasm—how, in fact, the first stage in independent nutrition is accomplished. When one liquid, say spirit, is poured into another, say water, the two gradually mix. If we suppose these liquids to consist of a number of molecules,* then, mixture may be taken to

---

* It may be well, once for all, to explain the sense in which the term "molecule" is here used. It is now generally assumed by physicists that every substance in nature is made up of excessively minute particles called atoms, which are indestructible. An atom cannot exist by itself, but in association with others. Such a group of atoms is called a "molecule." A molecule, therefore, is the smallest group of atoms capable of existing separately and independently. These molecules may be of different sizes in different cases, and they are believed to be so arranged as just not to touch, but to leave spaces between them; smaller in the case of a hard solid, wider in that of a liquid, still wider in that of a gas. The extent, moreover, of these interspaces may be increased or diminished by varying degrees of heat.

be the result of the displacement say of one molecule of water by one molecule of spirit, and so, throughout the whole quantity of liquid, there is displacement and replacement until at length equilibrium is restored and a thorough diffusion results. This power of diffusion does not always exist. The molecules of water and of oil will not mix or diffuse freely through each other. Water containing carbonic acid gas will not mix, in this sense of the term, with water containing acetate of lead; and when the attempt is made, chemical change is set up, the heretofore clear solutions—that containing the gas and that containing the lead—become when combined opaque and milky, owing to a chemical change, resulting in the formation of a white insoluble lead carbonate.

It may be a truism to say, that for the process of diffusion the liquids must be diffusible, but the fact must be carefully borne in mind in all questions relating to the feeding of plants. In the case of plants, the phenomenon of diffusion, or the gradual admixture of two liquids of different natures, is complicated by the presence of a membrane in the shape of the cell-wall. The water from the outside has to pass through the membrane to reach the protoplasm on the other side. Speaking broadly, there are no holes in the membrane through which the water can pass. Ingress is secured by that process of diffusion to which reference has just been made, and by virtue of which the molecules of the membrane and the molecules of the water shift and change places; the space that was occupied by a molecule of membrane is now occupied by a molecule of water, and *vice versa*. The access, therefore, of water into the interior of a closed cell is the result of the process of diffusion. Where two liquids mix without any intervening membrane, the mixture is called diffusion simply; where there is an intervening membrane, the diffusion process is known as "osmosis."

Protoplasm—Cells.—The raw material (the term is not quite accurate, but for illustration sake it may pass) is that very marvellous substance now called "protoplasm." We must leave it to chemists and microscopists to explain its composition and indicate its appearance. Suffice it here to call it, as Huxley did, "the physical basis of life." Without it, or when it is dead, the plant is dead too; with it the plant lives, without it it dies. It is a viscid, colorless, jelly-like substance, endowed with all those varied properties which constitute in the aggregate all that we can tangibly realize of the manifestations of life.

With few exceptions, which it is not necessary here to particularize, the protoplasm does not exist in one unbroken mass, but is contained in little membranous bags called "cells." These cells are of various shapes and sizes, and may undergo various modifications during the growth of the plant. They are large enough to be seen by the naked eye in the pulp of an orange, but usually they require the aid of the microscope to discern them. They are lengthened into tubes placed end to end to form conduits, or thickened into fibres. The cells, then, variously combined and modified, constitute what we have termed the fabric of the plant. Each living cell consists essentially of a certain proportion of protoplasm contained within a membranous bag or bladder, called technically the "cell-wall." There may be, and generally are, other things besides the protoplasm within the cell-wall, such, for instance, as a small ovoid body known as the "nucleus," and green coloring matter or "chlorophyll;" but these other things, important as they are, we may leave out of consideration for the present.

Every plant and every part of every plant is made up of cells such as have been mentioned. As a cell a plant begins its independent life; with and by cells it lives, grows, multiplies; by their decay it dies. It is, as has been said, the protoplasm, which is the essential agent in all these processes ; but, subject to a few exceptions, which need not now be specified, this protoplasm is always shut up within a cell-wall. Nor is it absolutely necessary that there should be more than one cell. Most plants with which the cultivator has to do consist of aggregations of such, but there are myriads of other plants which consist of but one cell; in such a case the cell is the plant, the plant is the cell. Now this is important, because it shows us that all the processes of life can be, and often are, carried on in one cell only, that is, by one fragment of protoplasm. Where the fabric becomes more complex, one cell is more or less dependent on another, but still there is always a measure of independence left to each individual cell. Were it not so, the scythe of the mower or the grazing of the sheep, by destroying a portion, would kill the entire plant.

It follows that the life-history of a plant is, in essence, the life-history of protoplasm and of its covering, the cell-wall; and hence it is that the microscopist or the chemist in the laboratory studying what goes on in isolated cells, placed as far as possible under uniform conditions, is really adopting the best means of investigating what takes place in the entire plant; a circumstance which the "practical man," so called, compelled to work in the field under such very different, more complex and much less definite conditions, finds it difficult to realize.

Conditions of Diffusion.—Diffusion, it will readily be understood from what has just been said, is not equal or alike in all cases ; it depends upon the extent to which the two liquids are diffusible, upon their different densities, upon temperature, and a variety of other conditions. So, in the case of osmosis, we have not only the nature of the two fluids to consider, but their relation to the membrane that separates them. The membrane may be much more permeable to one of the two fluids than to the other. Thus, in the case of a living cell, the membrane or wall is much more permeable to water than it is to protoplasm; and so it happens that, while water readily penetrates the membrane and diffuses itself in the protoplasm, protoplasm does not nearly so readily permeate the membrane as the water. Ingress of water is easy and of constant occurrence, egress of protoplasm is rare and exceptional.

Pure water or weak saline solutions, such as are generated in the soil under certain circumstances, pass readily through membrane—that is, the molecules of the one shift and change places with those of the other—while those of gummy or albuminoid substances like protoplasm do not. After a time, if there is no outlet for the water absorbed, or if it is not utilized within the plant in some way, absorption and diffusion cease, the cell becomes saturated with water, and until something happens to disarrange the balance, no more is absorbed. But, even in the case where the cell is saturated with water, it may still take up other liquids, because the diffusive power of those other liquids, in relation to the cell-wall and to the protoplasm, is different from that of water, and this absorption must go on in its way till saturation point is reached for each one of them, just as in the case of water. On the other hand, it may happen that the plant may be saturated with other substances, and incapable of taking up more of them, while at the same time pure water may be freely taken up.

Quantity absorbed.—Just so much and no more of each particular substance is absorbed, the exact quantity of each being regulated in all cases by the condition and requirements of the cells, their membranous walls, and their contents. Thus it happens that some particular substances may be found by the chemist to exist in large relative proportions in the plant, while the quantity in any given sample of the soil from which it must be derived, is sometimes so small as to elude detection. The plant in this case, or some part of it, is so greedy, if we may so say, for this particular substance, that it absorbs all within its reach, and stores it up in its tissues or uses it some way, the demand ensuring supply. On the other hand, the soil may contain a large quantity of some particular ingredient which is incapable of being absorbed, or which the plant does not or cannot make use of, and, in consequence, none is found within the plant. The supply is present, but there is no demand.

The different physical requirements of the plant supply also the explanation of the fact that different plants, grown in the same soil, supplied with the same food, yet vary so greatly in chemical composition. Thus, when wheat and clover are grown together, and afterwards analyzed, it is found that while lime is abundant in the clover, it is relatively in small quantity in the wheat; and silica, which is abundant in the wheat, is absent from the clover. Poisonous substances even may be absorbed, if they are of such a nature as to be capable of absorption; and so the plant may be killed by its own action—by suicide, as it were.

The entrance of water into the plant and the entrance of those soluble materials which a plant derives from the soil are therefore illustrations of the process of osmosis, and are subjected to all the conditions under which osmosis becomes possible, or under which it ceases to act. The study of these conditions is a question for the physicist, and the full explanation of them must be sought in works relating to physics. So the investigation of the substances which are absorbed with the water, of the food materials, and their transformations within the plant, is the work of the chemist, and their history must be sought in chemical books.

Continuous Changes in Plants.—In this place we must confine ourselves to the few passing references already made, but one thing we must strive to impress forcibly on the reader, because, if the notion is well grasped, it will enable him to understand plant life so much more vividly. We allude to the continual changes that are going on throughout the whole living fabric of the plant while in its active condition. Cell membrane, the protoplasm, the entire mass of liquid and solid constituents of which the plant consists, are, as we have seen, made up of molecules, each, as it were, with a life of its own, undergoing continual changes according to different circumstances, acting and reacting one upon another, so long as any active life remains. Active life, indeed, is ceaseless change; dormant life is a condition of equilibrium, more often talked about than realized—in fact, it is merely relative—it implies merely a lessened degree of activity. From this physical point of view the death of a cell is only a change, a rearrangement of particles, never, however, to be recombined into a new growing cell, as happens in the case of a still living cell in the full tide of growth and activity.

Nutritive Value of the Substances absorbed by Plants.—The importance of water may be judged from the fact that while succulent vegetables contain more than ninety per cent of water, timber felled in the driest time seldom contains less than forty per cent (Warington).

As to the nature of the saline substances, reference must, as has been said, be made to the "Chemistry of the Farm" and other works for full details. Suffice it here to say that certain of them, though always in relatively small proportions, are essential to the life of the plant; certain others, generally met with, though useful, are not indispensable. The former comprise salts of potash, magnesia, lime, iron, and in addition phosphorus and sulphur. The latter comprise salts of soda, silica, manganese, together with chlorine and occasionally other ingredients.

Of the salts just mentioned, the nitrates are of extreme importance, inasmuch as nitrogen is an essential constituent of protoplasm—without nitrogen there can be no protoplasm, without protoplasm there can be no plant. The nitrogen is supplied to the plants from the soil in the form either of nitrates (potassic nitrate, sodic nitrate), or of ammonia salts in which the nitrogen is in combination with hydrogen. The ammonia in the soil is made to combine with oxygen, and thus to form nitric acid, through the agency of minute organisms called "Bacteria," which, like the yeast fungus, act as ferments; and by their agency it is, as Mr. Warington has pointed out, in confirmation of the researches of Schloesing and Muntz, that the ammonia salts, which themselves are inert, or it may be harmful, get converted into useful nitrates. Ammonia salts applied to some soils do no good, because the needful germs or ferment bodies are not present in the soil; but where they do exist, they convert the useless into the useful, as before said. These bacteria occur in all fermenting material, such as farmyard dung, whose value as manure is in part accounted for by their presence and agency. It is probable in the future that just as the brewer uses his yeast to secure the conversion of starch into sugar, and the chemist "seeds" his solutions to effect the changes he wishes to bring about, and just as the gardener sows the spawn or germs of mushrooms in his mushroom bed, and obtains thereby a crop of succulent fungi, so the farmer may be able to apply to the soil the ferment-producing germs needed to change its quality, and render it available for plant food. When we have arrived at that point, manuring will be reduced to a science, and a pinch of the right material will be as efficient as a ton of our present compounds, the larger part of which are undoubtedly wasted under existing circumstances.

Potash salts are also essential, more so in some cases than in others. At Rothamsted, potash, after having been employed for a number of years as a manure-constituent on a certain grass plot, was discontinued; the produce, in consequence, rapidly declined, and the quantity of carbon fixed in the tissues of the plants proportionately diminished, although the amount of nitrogen absorbed was the same in the two cases. The presence, therefore, of an adequate supply of potash, in the soil, seems essential to the full assimilation of the carbon which is derived, as we shall presently see, from the air, in the form of carbonic acid gas. It is believed from recent experiments that without potash no starch can be formed; and starch, as we shall see hereafter, is of primary importance in the nutrition of the plant. In any case the value of potash manures for increasing the yield of certain crops, particularly potatoes, is a fact beyond dispute.

Sulphur and phosphorus are also derived from the soil as sulphates and phosphates. Both occur in association with the albuminoid contents of the protoplasm; and phosphorus seems specially needful in the formation of the pollen—the fertilizing powder in the flowers—and in the ripening of seeds, while its effect on the growth of turnips is familiar to all practical men.

Iron is essential to the formation of leaf-green—"chlorophyll"—and chlorophyll is essential to the production of starch; hence iron in some shape is essential to plants, and it also is supplied from the soil in the form of saline solutions.

What precise function lime plays in the plant's economy is not known; but indirectly it is of importance as a means of introducing phosphorus and other essential ingredients. At Rothamsted, in two of the plots upon which barley has been grown for thirty years in succession, a mineral manure with nitrogen has been applied; but in the one case lime has been added, in the other (otherwise treated exactly in the same way) no lime has been added. The plants on the plot without the lime are always of a darker green color, but they are relatively deficient in carbon. Under equal conditions, it is seen that the amount of carbon assimilated from the atmosphere in the manner to be hereafter mentioned is directly dependent on the amount of available nitrogen, which latter is derived from the soil—(Lawes and Gilbert).

It must not be forgotten that the substances we have mentioned, as well as others not alluded to, though possibly not directly concerned in the nutrition of the plant, yet are so indirectly by causing changes in the soil, by rendering some matters soluble and capable of osmotic absorption which would not be so without their aid, by storing up and preventing the waste of ingredients useful as plant food, and so forth; but these matters pertain rather to the physical and chemical history of the soil, on which account they may be passed over here without further mention.

Principles of Manuring.—The few remarks we have thought it right to make as to the nature of the substances absorbed with the water from the soil have an important bearing on the theory and practice of manuring. The nitrogenous and the saline substances are taken from the soil, used up in the plant, and removed in the crop. The annual produce of hay on unmanured land at Rothamsted, has been found to be about two thousand five hundred and seventy-six pounds per acre, over an average of twenty-five years, the range of variation according to season having been from nine hundred to four thousand three hundred and sixty-eight pounds. On the other hand, the most highly manured plot has yielded for the same period an average of seven thousand one hundred and sixty-eight pounds of hay per acre, varying in separate years from four thousand four hundred and eighty to eight thousand nine hundred and sixty pounds, according to season. These figures will suffice to illustrate the amount of food derived from the soil and from the atmosphere, and the beneficial effects of suitable climatal conditions. The decline not only of produce, but also in mineral and nitrogenous ingredients in the soil, in the case of the continuously unmanured plots at Rothamsted, is very marked. To insure continued fertility, therefore, and obviate exhaustion, some restitution must be made; and this is effected by the addition at the right time, in the right condition, and in the right quantities, of an appropriate manure; or the exhaustion may be compensated by suitable rotation, or the growth in alternate periods of plants having different requirements, as wheat after potatoes or clover after wheat.

Apparent Power of Selection, how Explained.—The circumstance that certain crops are specially benefited by particular manures, though they contain relatively little of the substance in their composition, would seem to indicate the existence of a power of selection, as also would the fact that plants of such very different constitutions grow on the same soil, but these facts are better explained by the varying osmotic conditions of the plants. Cereal crops and grasses generally are, for instance, specially benefited by nitrogenous manures, though they contain relatively little nitrogen as compared with clover and other leguminous crops, but which, although they contain so large a proportion of nitrogen in their constitution, are not particularly benefited by nitrogenous manures. Beet roots and potatoes, which contain a considerable proportion of potash in their constitution, are, nevertheless, not proportionately benefited by the application of potash manures, though they are so to some extent. These cases show that, by virtue of the varying osmotic and digestive powers already mentioned, the plants in question take what they want, and when they want it, and are not induced to take more by the addition of larger supplies. They further show the errors that may arise from the farmer acting too implicitly on the results obtained by the chemist in the laboratory. If he followed the indications of the chemist unchecked by other experience, he would apply to his land what was really not required by the crop. Thus Messrs. Lawes and Gilbert tell us that the exact composition of the crops is no direct guide to the description and amount of manurial constituents that will be most effective, thus although wheat removes more phosphoric acid from the soil than does barley, yet the application of the phosphate is more beneficial to the barley than to the wheat. They conclude, then, that it is not necessary to supply to the land all the constituents that have been removed from it, or that would be contained in the crops it is wished to grow, but that we should supply all or some, more or less, according to circumstances.

CHAPTER II.

NUTRITION (*Continued*).—THE MACHINERY.

Roots: their nature.—Root-cap.—Root-hairs.—Root action.—Absorption.—Leaves and leaf action.—Chlorophyll.—Absorption of fluid and gases.—Leaf work by day and by night.—Oxidation and De-oxidation.—Carnivorous plants.—Transpiration.—Circumstances propitious to it.—The stem and its work.—Its characteristics and varieties.—Buds.—Branches.—Tubers.—Bulbs.—Uses of the stem.—Ascent of liquids.—Sap currents.

Roots: Their Nature, Etc.—So far as regards the absorption of those food materials derived from the soil by the means above-mentioned, the root and its sub-divisions are the agents through which the absorption takes place. It is not necessary to allude to the various forms and modifications of roots which form the study of the botanist further than to say that their manifold differences of form depend chiefly on the relative proportion that the body of the root bears to its branches. If, as in a "tap-root," like a carrot, the body is large, the branches are small; if, as in the "fibrous root" of a grass, the body is small, the branches are numerous and long.

In ordinary language a great many things are called roots which are not strictly so. For most people all parts of the plant situate below the surface of the ground are roots or portions of roots. Botanists, having regard alike to the origin, mode of growth, structure, and uses of roots, are enabled to define roots partly by positive, partly by negative characters. Thus roots originate beneath the surface, that is from within the tissues of the plant (endogenous), and force their way out through the rind, as contrasted with branches and leaves which originate on the surface (exogenous). The extreme tip of the root, and of its sub-divisions, is furnished with a minute "root-cap" of dead tissue pushed off from the tip as it grows, as the feathers of a bird are removed during the moulting season. No such cap exists at the end of a branch or leaf. Again, while it is the office of a stem or branch to produce leaves or scales, which are the representatives of leaves, no root proper, as a rule, produces leaves or flowers.

Botanists make a distinction between "true roots"— which are the direct outgrowth from the original "radicle" of the germinating seedling, and, in fact constitute its direct continuation—and "adventitious" roots, which spring from the stem and branches, and which are only indirectly derived from the primary root. For our present purpose the distinction is unimportant.

The root of a plant and its branches have different forms and subserve different purposes. Whatever food is taken up from the soil is taken up by them. They act as stays and holdfasts, they serve as storehouses of nourishment. Their form varies according to their use, their needs, the competition with other roots, the conditions under which they have to grow, and other circumstances, not forgetting the heritage bequeathed to them by their predecessors from generation to generation, for, like all parts of the plant—like the plant itself—the root is the product of what has gone before, adapted and modified by the exigencies of the present.

In this place we have to consider the roots chiefly in their character as absorbent organs. The one function common to all roots is absorption. They may have other offices to fulfil, and they have very varied forms; but when we come to consider the main function of the root, then we find simplicity and relative uniformity of structure. The thick, woody limb of an elm root, as we see it exposed in a hedge-bank from which the soil has fallen, is no organ of absorption; the thick "bulbs" (so-called) of a turnip or a beet, are not organs of absorption; neither are these latter, any more than the tubers of potatoes, strictly speaking, roots. Our best and truest conception of a root as an organ of absorption is that of a single fibril or of a dense mass of the finest fibrils—root-branches no thicker than a hair. These fibrils grow in length close to their tips, the actual tip being covered with a thin extinguisher-like cap of dead tissue—the root-cap already mentioned, and which serves as a shield to the softer tissues within. The structure is of the simplest, merely layers of cells such as before described, arranged in more or less longitudinal ranks, the cells themselves delicate and thin-walled. The fineness of the root-fibril, its growth near the tip, its wonderful power of motion, are all well adapted to permit of the fibril making its way between the particles of soil, and extracting nourishment from the fluid surrounding them. We have only to examine the root of a wheat plant, or still better of a perennial pasture grass, to see how perfectly this is accomplished. Under such circumstances the root-fibrils form a dense wig, as it were, of feeding threads which occupy the soil so thoroughly that the soil is held together by them. It is easy to see that although the absorbent power of each thread is infinitesimal, yet in the aggregate it must be very large. Fine as they often are, these root-fibrils are very frequently, but not always, provided with yet finer "root-hairs." These are extremely minute threads emerging from the superficial cells of the root, in the vicinity of, but not exactly at, their tips. When their growth is stimulated by the presence of moisture or suitable plant food, they often occur in such numbers as to form a dense cobweb-like investment to the roots.

Root Action—What the Roots do.—It has been proved by repeated experiments that the absorption of liquid food (no solid matter can in any case be absorbed) takes place towards the lower end of the root-fibrils, and by means of these root-hairs when they are present. The upper portions of the fibril do not act as absorbent organs, the root hairs do not exist in this part of the root, the structure of which becomes gradually less and less adapted for absorption, so that the actual space in each fibril devoted to absorption is relatively small in relation to its length. The remainder of the fibril acts as a conduit for the transmission of the absorbed fluids upward from cell to cell by osmosis and imbibition, and as a holdfast.

The passage of the insoluble matters in the soil into the root is effected by an acid liquid produced by the root-hair or cell in consequence of its contact with the particle of soil, aided by the water in the soil. This acid fluid saturates the cell walls, corrodes, and effects the solution of the surface of the particle of the soil in contact with the fibril or root-hair. No passage of acid fluid out of the cell takes place, root excretions having no existence; but the corrosive, and as it were digestive, action above mentioned, is due solely to the absolute contact of the cell of the root with the particle of the soil.

The soil, therefore, is not to be looked on as containing so much liquid food ready for instant use; that may be so as regards water, but for other substances the digestive action of the roots is necessary.

In addition to the absorption of liquids as just detailed, roots have the power of freely absorbing the oxygen gas contained in the soil, and if a supply of oxygen be cut off, the roots die from suffocation. One use, therefore, of the plowing and harrowing operations is to keep the soil open and permeable, and thus allow the access of oxygen to the roots.

On the other hand, roots do not absorb carbonic acid gas nor exhale oxygen as the leaves do—in the sunlight—but they do give off carbonic acid gas, which, with the aid of water, converts the insoluble carbonates of the soil into soluble bicarbonates, and exercises a similar power of solution in the case of phosphates.

Leaves and Leaf Action.—The two great factors in the feeding of the plant are the roots and the leaves. The soil supplies to the roots, as we have seen, water in large quantities, gases, earthly and saline substances ; but the air is an equally important source of nourishment, or even more so, since there are rootless plants, and plants which receive no part of their food directly from the soil, while no plant can exist without air, and no plant that is of direct importance to the cultivator can live without light. We insert the word "direct" because there is a whole group of plants which can thrive in the absence of light, but these form no part of the ordinary crops of a farm. Indirectly, however, as has been pointed out, in considering the agency of bacteria as ferments in the soil, these organisms to whose career light is not essential may be of the greatest consequence to cultivators ; and it is probable that the future will show us much more fully how great is our indebtedness to them. For our present purpose, we have to deal with plants producing leaves, to point out some of the work which the leaves do, and to give some indication of how they do it.

Unlike the root, which originates from within the substance of the plant and breaks its way out to the surface, the leaf, as has been stated, is a direct production from the surface of the stem or branch. It is one of the characteristics of a root not to produce leaves ; it is one of the attributes of the stem and its subdivisions to clothe themselves with these appendages.

In form. texture, size, the leaf presents infinite variety. Sometimes it is a mere dry scale, sometimes a thick, fleshy excrescence ; now it offers a broad, banner-like surface, now it is reduced to the form and dimensions of a needle. Sometimes it is all in one piece, the "blade" being unbroken at the edge, or variously notched and indented; at other times the blade is made up of few or of an infinite number of separate segments or leaflets. If the blade is in one piece, it is "simple," as the leaf of wheat; if in many pieces, as the leaf of clover, sainfoin, or tares, it is "compound." Very often it has a stalk or "petiole," sometimes it has none. Sometimes it has appendages at its base called "stipules," well seen in vetches or clover; while the leaves of all grasses, including all the cereals, are provided with a little membranous tongue or outgrowth from the junction of the sheathing stalk of the leaf with the blade, which is called a "ligule," and which, though often overlooked, is of some moment to the grazing farmer, as affording one means of distinguishing useful from useless grasses. Further than this we need not go at present in speaking of the form and general appearance of leaves. Nor need we enter very deeply into the minutiæ of their structure. All ordinary leaves are flat plates of cells of various shapes variously arranged, and traversed by fibrous bundles. These bundles consist of long, tapering cells or fibres filled with woody or other matter, and of rows of similar cells placed end to end in rows, the partitions between the cells being removed, so that they form continuous tubes. There are many kinds of "vessels," but all of them originate from cells. The fibro-vascular bundles, with their wood-cells, bast-cells, and vessels, constitute what are commonly termed the veins of the leaf. Covering over this mass of cells and vessels is a skin or epidermis, consisting of flattened cells usually placed in accurate contact on the upper surface of the leaf, but below, so modified in shape and position as to leave a number of pores or openings called "stomata," the number, arrangement, size, and form of which vary very much in different plants; suffice it here to say that they are in general very numerous. So far, then, there is little difference to be noted between the structural elements of a leaf and those of a root. The root is more or less cylindric, the leaf is more or less flat; but the essential structures, though differently arranged, are pretty much the same, with one or two notable exceptions. The root has no breathing pores or stomata, and the contents of its constituent cells are so far different from those of the leaves that they contain no green coloring matter.

Chlorophyll.—The main and specially important characteristic of the leaf (and of all the green parts of plants), so far as their life-work is concerned, is the presence in the cells of the green matter called "chlorophyll." With and by its agency the leaf can do work impossible to be done otherwise; work, the measure of which determines the health and vigor of the plant, the default of which ensures its death. It is true that chemists and physicists have not yet unravelled all the mysteries of chlorophyll, and there remains a doubt whether it is the potent agent it has hitherto been supposed to be, or whether the power does not reside in some other agent mixed with it. Into these questions we cannot here enter. Whatever be the actual truth of the matter, the transcendent importance of chlorophyll, and of all that its presence implies, is universally admitted. It must suffice to say that chlorophyll is a green, waxy substance, occurring in certain of the cells mixed with their protoplasmic contents. In amount and appearance it varies in different cases and under varying circumstances. It does not occur in all the cells of the leaf, but chiefly or only in those on the upper surface, and which are therefore the most directly exposed to the action of the rays of the sun.

Feeding by Leaves.—We are now in a position to understand the nutritive process as it is carried on by the leaves, and our first enquiry is as to what they feed on—what is the nature of the food they take in? In the first place, it is clear that they can take in no solid matter. The pores or stomata already alluded to are the only openings by which such matter could get into the interior of the leaf; and we know, from experience, that if these pores get blocked, the leaf suffers rather than gains. Moreover, the cells, bounding the aperture, open and close according to the condition of moisture of the atmosphere, and at any rate, when closed, they could admit no solid matter.

Absorption of Water.—As to fluids, it is proved that leaves, under certain circumstances, and when there is no structural provision to prevent it (as there often is) can and do absorb, not only watery vapor, but the fluid itself. This happens more especially when the plant is flagging from the rapid exhalation of moisture, and from deficient root supply, and it affords an explanation of the benefit plants derive from the deposit of dew after a hot and drying day. Still, the absorption of water by means of the root seems to be generally of more consequence than that by the leaf, so that the entrance of water by the leaf may, for our purposes, be passed over without further mention.

Absorption and Exhalation of Gases.—There remains gaseous food. It has been shown that the root absorbs gases, as oxygen; but in this respect, as also in the absorption of other gases, the root is surpassed by the leaf. The paramount function of the leaf is the absorption and assimilation of carbon. Carbon, as such, does not exist in the atmosphere, unless, indeed, as an impurity in the air of towns, and a very prejudicial one to plants. It is in the form of carbonic acid gas—a combination of carbon and oxygen—that it is found in the atmosphere, but only in small proportion compared with the other constituents. In the plant carbon exists in much larger proportion than any other ingredient, with the sole exception of water. It forms, in fact, about fifty per cent of the dry matter of plants left behind after the water and gases have been expelled by heat. This large quantity of carbon has to be taken up in the form of carbonic acid by the leaves. It is a moot point whether any carbon is taken up by the roots, but, if any, it is only a small proportion. In any given volume or quantity of air, the proportion of carbonic acid is very minute, so that the leaves must be very active in securing and utilizing all that comes within their reach.

What Leaves do in the Light.—Direct experiments have shown that this appropriation of carbonic acid is effected by the agency of the green coloring matter or chlorophyll when exposed to the action of light. In the dark no such appropriation takes place. The plant feeds, so far as its carbon is concerned, on the carbonic acid of the air through the agency of sunlight and of chlorophyll. At least two-thirds of the chlorophyll itself consists of carbon in association with a small proportion of oxygen and hydrogen, and a still smaller quantity of nitrogen. The carbonic acid thus introduced into the plant does not remain as such, but its constituent carbon is retained in the plant for its own purposes, while the oxygen gas is eliminated. The bubbles of gas that rise from a water weed in a pond when exposed to the sun consist of oxygen chiefly, and it has been shown that the amount of oxygen gas given off is about equal to that of the carbonic acid gas absorbed. Hydrogen and oxygen, the absorbed water, are, it is said, assimilated by the plant simultaneously with the carbon.

The first result of this assimilation, chemists tell us, is the formation of a soluble substance, "glucose," allied both to starch and to sugar, and which, or a portion of which, becomes starch, and is stored up for future use in that form. No starch is formed in an atmosphere purposely deprived of carbonic acid by the experimenter, even if the cell be exposed to the light. Moreover, any starch that may have been previously formed disappears under such circumstances, just as it would do in darkness, where the plant is dependent on its reserve stores for its nourishment, and not on those which it procures directly for itself when exposed to light in an atmosphere in which carbonic acid gas forms a part. The changes in question are presumed to take place, not in the protoplasm itself, but in the chlorophyll grains; at any rate, it is in them that the starch first makes its appearance. It is certain, also, that only cells which contain chlorophyll — and then only when exposed to light — can directly assimilate carbon. Cells without chlorophyll, such as those of fungi, obtain their carbon by more indirect and complex means. The vital importance of the exposure of the leaves to sunlight might be inferred from the bending of the stems and branches to the light, and placing of the mobile leaves at such an angle as to receive the full benefit of the sun's rays—matters which will be spoken of further on.

What the Leaves do in Darkness.—Inhalation of Oxygen.—In darkness (as well as under the influence of light, in the case of those cells that do not contain chlorophyll) changes go on of a different character to those just described. There is, in fact, a constant elimination of carbonic acid gas, and a corresponding absorption and retention of oxygen gas. The interchange of these gases has been compared to the corresponding changes in the case of the respiration of animals; but doubts have been thrown on the existence of any direct connection between the absorption of oxygen and the emission of carbonic acid, in plants, because it has been shown that a green leaf placed in darkness and in an atmosphere deprived of oxygen nevertheless exhales carbonic acid, the emission of which under such circumstances cannot of course be connected with any corresponding inhalation of oxygen.

Though going on constantly, the energy of the oxidizing process is much less than that of the opposite deoxidizing process, carried on when the chlorophyll cells are exposed to the light. Deprived of oxygen, the movements of the protoplasm, the movements of the roots and of the leaves cease, other manifestations of activity are put a stop to, and the plant dies of suffocation. Moreover, it has been shown that each cell consumes its own supply of oxygen, and if that fails it will die, even though adjoining cells be provided with the gas. In this particular then the cells act, not in concert, but individually (Van Tieghem). It is not essential that the oxygen should be in a free state; it may be utilized by plants from a compound containing oxygen, and from which it may easily be obtained. An instance of this is afforded in the case of the disease of animals known as "charbon," which is now known to be caused by the existence in the blood of the animal affected of a microscopic plant (Bacillus anthracis), which lives in the blood, and which, not finding sufficient oxygen in its serum or liquid portion, decomposes the matter contained in the red corpuscles and utilizes the oxygen they afford. To live itself, it deprives the creature in which it is established of its oxygen, and thus not only kills it by suffocation, but eventually cuts off its own supply of food.

The effect of depriving a plant which contains glucose of its oxygen is to convert that glucose into alcohol. Thus fermented liquors, such as beer, wine, etc., owe the alcohol they contain to the temporary cutting off of the supply of oxygen to the ferment, in consequence of which the glucose they contain becomes converted into alcohol.

Carnivorous Plants, Parasites.—The leaves of certain plants are endowed under certain circumstances with a power of digesting and absorbing animal substances placed in contact with them. When a minute fragment of meat, for instance, is placed upon the leaf of a drosera, or sundew, the tentacle-like glandular hairs of the plant bend over to grasp the intruding morsel, a peculiar digestive fluid is formed as a result of the contact—just as the gastric juice in the human stomach is secreted when food enters that organ—and this fluid effects the solution of the meat, the nutritive solution so formed being absorbed and applied to the benefit of the plant. To common observation the actual gain to the plant by this method of feeding may appear slight, or even none; but the more delicate tests applied by the botanist have sufficed to prove, not only that the processes just mentioned really do go on, but also that they are beneficial to the plant, and contribute to the formation of more numerous and more robust seedlings. The *rationale* of this mode of obtaining nutrition seems somewhat analogous to that in the root, where also the acid fluid with which the cell-wall is permeated, when it comes into contact with the particles of soil, determines their solution and renders them fit for absorption into the plant. Practically this admittedly exceptional mode of nutrition by the leaf might seem of little moment, but it is probable that in the future direct nutrition by this means will be shown to be of much greater importance than it appears to be at present. In any case, the fact that ammonia-solutions and ammonia-vapors are absorbed by leaves with increased manifestations of vital activity, renders this mode of feeding a matter of some consequence to the agriculturist; and the escape of ammoniacal vapor from the muck-heap may not after all be the wasteful operation it is usually supposed to be—that is, if the circumstances are such that plants can avail themselves of the exhaled vapor.

It is a very remarkable fact that fluids which do not contain nitrogen do not give rise to the movements of the leaves, the changes in the protoplasm, the formation of a digestive fluid, and other consequences, which Darwin has discussed in his work on "Insectivorous Plants." Mere mechanical irritation of the leaves is not sufficient to ensure the formation of the ferment requisite for digestion. The different effects of salts of soda and of potash, in the case of the leaves of drosera, are also suggestive, for while soda-salts give rise to the physiological activity in the leaves, potash salts do not do so, and some of them are even poisonous. Neither the one nor the other is poisonous to the roots, unless applied in very large quantities. Phosphate of ammonia and phosphate of soda act with remarkable vigor on the leaves, while phosphate of potash is quite inert, the activity in the former cases being probably due to the phosphorus.

It would thus appear that while almost all plants absorb the inorganic elements, including their nitrogen, from the soil, and derive their carbon from the atmosphere, there are others, such as drosera, which digest and absorb nitrogenous matters by means of their leaves. Such plants can even extract nitrogenous matter from pollen, seeds, and bits of leaves (Darwin). Other plants absorb ammonia by means of the hairs covering their leaves, and this class is probably more numerous than the foregoing. Others, again, have no faculty of digesting by their leaves, though they absorb solutions of decaying animal matter by their means. Some, such as the bird's nest orchis, feed on the decay of vegetable matter, and are themselves nearly or quite destitute of chlorophyll. Lastly, there is the class of true parasites, such as the broom-rapes (*Orobanche*) and dodders (*Cuscuta*), which affix themselves to living plants, and being themselves destitute of chlorophyll, are unable to live, except at the expense of the plants upon which they grow.

Transpiration of Water.—There is a large absorption of water, as has been said, by means of the root, and in some cases, at any rate, there is an absorption of the same fluid or vapor by means of the leaves. On the other hand, there is a loss of water or watery vapor from the surface, which is sometimes so profuse as to cause the plant to wither and flag. We have only to place some leaves in a cool tumbler, and expose them to the light, to see the condensed water on the sides of the glass. The quantity of watery vapor emitted in sunlight by the green surfaces of plants is enormous, and it has been shown experimentally that it is the chlorophyll which is largely concerned in this outflow, for where that substance is deficient and wanting, transpiration of fluid is proportionately reduced or stopped. But while bright light, such as that furnished by the red and yellow ray of the solar spectrum, is most efficacious in stimulating the decomposition of carbonic acid, it is the blue ray which specially favors transpiration of the fluid. A high degree of temperature, as might be expected, favors transpiration, as does also a dry state of the atmosphere. The condition of the plant, its age, and other circumstances are also important agents in regulating the amount of transpiration.

Some idea of the amount of water given off may be gleaned from some experiments made by Sir John Lawes, and recorded in the "Journal" of the Horticultural Society for 1850, thus—During one hundred and seventy-two days, March 19 to September 7, the total weight of water given off from small flower pots containing plants, grown without manure, was as follows:—

	Grains.
Wheat	112,527
Barley	120,025
Beans	112,231
Peas	109,082

or, say, an average loss for each pot for the whole period of over one hundred thousand grains. To show the effect of the season, it may be said that the average daily loss in grains in the case of flower pots containing plants of wheat grown in unmanured soil, was:

	Grains.
March 19 to 28	14.3
March 28 to April 28	40.9
April 28 to May 25	162.4
May 25 to June 28	1177.4
June 28 to July 28	1535.3
July 28 to August 11	1101.4
August 11 to September 7	230.9

Barley lost more in April and May than the wheat, and more also in July and August. Beans lost much less than either of the cereals, the amount increasing regularly to June to July, and diminishing in August. Peas evaporated less than beans, especially in June. The results obtained from the plants grown with various manures were less uniform, and need not here be cited, the object being merely to illustrate the large quantity of water evaporated and its gradual increase with the development and growth of the plant and the advance of the season. While the precise effect of any particular manure in promoting either absorption or transpiration is not fully known, it has been shown that the alternate use of pure water and of manure water has resulted in a large proportionate amount of water being absorbed and transpired by the plant, and a greater development of the plant than is the case where either fluid is applied alone (Vesque).

Summary.—The main functions of the leaf may, therefore, be stated to be the reception and emission of gases —now this, now that, according as it is exposed to light or darkness—and the absorption and emission of watery vapor. The result of all these varied processes now acting together and in unison—at other times in antagonism as it were—is the nutrition of the plant, the building up of its structure, the formation of most of those ingredients which render a plant sightly or useful. The importance of these processes may be summed up in the words of an eminent physiologist ("Gardeners' Chronicle," 1881, Feb. 5, p. 169) :—" All the labor of the plant by which out of air, water, and a pinch of divers salts scattered in the soil, it builds up leaf and stem and roots, and puts together material for seed or bud or bulb, is wrought and wrought only by the green cells which give greenness to leaf and branch or stem. . . . We may say of the plant that the green cells of the green leaves are the blood thereof. As the food which an animal takes remains a mere burden until it is transmuted into blood, so the material which the roots bring to the plant is mere dead food until the cunning toil of a chlorophyll-holding cell has passed into it the quickening sunbeam. Take away from a plant even so much as a single green leaf, and you rob it of so much of its very life blood." A warning this against the premature removal of leaves, as when leaves are taken from the bulbs of our mangels before they have completed their work of formation and accumulation.

In this, and other matters, however, the cultivator often has to make a compromise, and act as is best for himself under the particular circumstances of the time. It is not the good of the plant that he seeks in the first instance, but only in so far as it contributes to his own profit ; and although in principle every injury needlessly inflicted on a plant must in the long run be injurious, it may well be and often is the case that the injury to the plant is compensated for by other conditions, and that, in case of difficulties on both sides, it is wisest to choose the least of two.

The Stem and its Work.—As the leaves, whatever their form, are nothing but outgrowths from the stem, and as no leaf exists except it be borne upon a stem, so it would have been more in the natural order of things if mention had been made of it before the leaves. As regards the nutrition of the plant, however, the stem plays but a secondary part, as compared either with the root or the leaves, and on this account it may not inappropriately be considered after them.

Botanically, any part of the plant that produces leaves, or the representatives of leaves, is considered to be stem. The root, inasmuch as it bears neither scales nor leaves, is not stem; the "root-stock," inasmuch as it does bear scales and leaves, is truly a stem, even though it may be beneath ground. The long, creeping runners of "twitch" (*Triticum repens*) are stems, so are the similar parts in thistles and bear-bind (*Convolvulus arvensis*). The bulbs of kohl rabi are clearly stems, for they bear leaves, or the scars where leaves have once been. Beet roots, mangels, radishes, turnips, parsnips, partake of the nature of roots and of stems; that is to say, their lower, tapering extremities are unquestionably roots; their thick upper end, surmounted by a crown of leaves, is as unquestionably stem. There are anatomical differences —such as the presence of a root-cap, the absence of stomata in a root, and differences in the mode of growth— between roots and stems, but they are not material to our present purpose. It will be seen, from what has been above said, that the definition of a stem (or of a branch, which is only a subdivision of a stem), as that part of the plant told off to bear leaves, admits of very wide differences of form. We have already alluded to some of these differences, according as the stem is above or below ground, covered with mere scale-leaves, or bedecked like a timber tree with true leaves. The pasture grasses and cereals have almost all hollow erect, knotted stems; the sedges, which resemble the grasses so much, have mostly angular unjointed stems. The clovers have a thick stock giving off branches which trail along the ground. The hop coils around the supporting pole by means of its climbing stem. Then there are the differences in duration associated with corresponding differences in texture and internal construction. There are the so-called annual stems, which would lie down, even if they were not cut down after one season's growth; there are the perennial stems, like those of fruit or timber trees or shrubs, and the duration of whose existence may be counted by years, and often by centuries. Then, again, there is an intermediate class of cases where the rootstock remains below-ground for a period long enough to justify the term perennial, while the branches or shoots die down after the seed is ripe, or are killed to the ground by a touch of frost, as in the common nettles.

Buds, Branches, Tubers, Etc.—The branches or subdivisions of a stem originate as buds or "eyes," which are placed at the free ends of the stem or of its branches, or which originate from the side of the stem or branch, in what is called the "axil" of a leaf, or of a leaf-scale, the axil being the angle formed by the base of the leaf at the point where it springs from the stem. The traces of their origin are often lost as the plant grows, but the rule is, as it has been stated, subject to a few exceptions of no moment for our present purpose. It is not usual for a bud to be borne in the axil of every leaf, far from it, but this is the place where the side-buds when they do exist are almost sure to be found. The shoots which "tiller" up from the base of the stems of the wheat originate as buds from the axils of the lower leaves, while the upper ones are destitute of them. When a tree is "pollarded," a large crop of buds makes its appearance; and the multiplication of some weeds, like thistles and bindweed, after their stocks have been cut through with the hoe at insufficient depths below the surface, is due to a like formation of buds.

The tuber of the potato may be mentioned under this heading. Though commonly called a root, because it happens to grow below-ground, it is clearly a stem, because it is provided with "eyes," which eyes, as may be seen when the tuber begins to sprout, are nothing but buds. A tuber, then, is a portion of the stem of the plant, in which the tissues become thickened and filled with nutritive matter (in this case starch), which is provided with buds, and which, when once fully formed, is separated from the parent haulm or stem by the gradual decay and death of the latter. A tuber of this kind fulfils in the economy of the plant much the same purpose as the seed; and hence the term "seed potato," though far from correct in a technical sense, conveys, nevertheless, a not wholly incorrect idea.

A "bulb," such as that of an onion, is a portion of the stem modified for the same purposes as the tuber; but whereas in a tuber the stem itself is swollen, and the leaves reduced to the merest scales, in a bulb the conditions are reversed: the fleshy scales of an onion bulb are really the bases of the leaves, as any one may see who will examine an onion in growth, while the stem itself is reduced to a mere, flat, and not very thick plate, from the sides of which emerge the leaves. The term bulb, as applied to such a root as the turnip, is inaccurate.

These illustrations, taken from plants most familiar to the cultivator, will suffice to show the general character of the stem and its subdivisions, and will indicate the great extent of variation there is in its outward characteristics. The inward conformation of the stem varies according to the nature of the plant—its age and the purpose it fulfils. The structure of the stem of a timber tree and that of a potato tuber—both, as we have seen, forms of stems—are naturally different. In the one case thin-walled cells filled with starch predominate, in the other wood-cells and fibres filled with woody matter are most abundant. Still, great as are the differences in the manner in which the structural elements are arranged in different cases, those elements are precisely the same as those mentioned as existing in the root and in the leaf; and the structure of a stem, however ultimately complicated, is in the first instance quite simple, being merely an aggregation of cells. Another stem, of very different general appearance it may be, began in precisely the same way. It is only necessary here to allude in passing to the variations in internal structure, according to circumstances, as they must necessarily be referred to again when dealing with the office of the stem and its mode of growth.

Uses of the Stem—the Sap.—Having gained a general notion of the nature and construction of the stem, it is necessary to enquire as to its office. What does it do for the plant? The answer to this may in a measure be gleaned from what has been said as to the office of the leaves. The necessity for their exposure to sunlight has been shown, and to ensure this exposure, and to provide that one leaf shall overshadow and interfere with its neighbor as little as possible, the stem lengthens, and the leaves are thrown off, now on this side, now on that, so that each shall do its own work under the most favorable circumstances, and hinder its neighbor to the least possible degree. One leaf would not be of much use, but the aggregation of many produces a timber tree.

One leaf's work would probably not suffice to build up a grain of wheat, the aggregation of them serves to form a sheaf of plump ears. The stem, in fact, is the agency by which the work of individual leaves is combined and concentrated for the general benefit of the plant. Each separate leaf, like each separate cell, has a life of its own, and to some extent is independent of every other leaf; but, if they are to be of any use to the plant as a whole, there must be a co-operation. The stem and its branches supply the means for this co-operation. Moreover, there must also be co-operation between the root and the leaves. Root action by itself would not benefit the plant, even if it were practicable. Leaf action, apart from the root, would soon come to an end. The leaves by their copious evaporating surfaces act as suckers to draw up the water from the soil by the agency of the roots. Thus as the stem is the agent between leaf and leaf, so it is the go-between betwixt the roots and the leaves. Apart, then, from its function of bearing leaves and flowers in such numbers and in such manner as shall secure the greatest benefit to the plant under the circumstances in which it is placed—apart also from its office of storing up food for future use—we have to consider how it is that the stem acts as the go-between betwixt the root and the leaves, and between the leaves themselves.

Ascent of Liquids.—It is certain that liquids, chiefly water, and gases, mount up from the soil to the leaves. How they enter the root has been explained, and their passage up the stem against the direction of gravity may be accounted for on like principles of diffusion. There are, however, various circumstances which aid the upward flow of the liquid. The distended condition of the cells and the swollen state of their walls must exercise pressure on the contained fluids, the direction of which is mostly from below upwards. This pressure, or squeezing process, is augmented by the swaying of the branches or the movements of the leaves. Even more powerful must be the effect of the atmospheric pressure urging up the liquid to fill the place of that evaporated from the leaf surface. This upward current is naturally most active at the period of growth, and the channels through which it flows are necessarily those where the conditions for osmosis are most propitious. In proportion, therefore, as the cells become filled with woody or earthy material does the current become less. As the straw ripens or the timber hardens by the formation of wood in its cells, so does the flow of liquid diminish, the leaves in their turn and degree become obstructed and fall, and the current, deprived of their stimulus, becomes feeble.

But while in thus alluding to some of the duties of the stem, we have had to note the existence during the period of growth of a current of liquid whose general direction is upward, it is necessary to point out that the direction is not exclusively upward, but that it is manifested in whatever direction the resistance is least and where growth may be going on most actively at the time. Again, it is necessary to guard against the still prevalent fallacy attaching to the use of the word "sap." That term was first employed when it was imagined that a regular circulation of fluid took place in plants from root to leaf, and from leaf back to root—just as in animals the blood courses from the heart through the arteries to the capillaries, and back from the capillaries to the heart by the veins. In the case of the higher animals there is a continuous series of tubes to convey the fluid, and that fluid is uniformily arterial or venous. It is quite otherwise with plants; there is no continuous tube or set of tubes, and there is no fluid of uniformily the same composition throughout. Near the root the juice of the plant has one composition, near the leaf another.

The word "sap," then, though convenient, must not be used or conceived of as indicating the existence of a current absolutely fixed in its direction or uniform in its composition. In other words, it has but a remote analogy to the blood, with which it is so often compared. There is an upward current of watery fluid, well marked in spring, there are downward and cross currents varying in direction and intensity according to the requirements of the growing tissues and their conformation. These have only indirect connection with the main upward flow just referred to.

CHAPTER III.

GROWTH.

Growth and extension.—Growth of cells.—Growing points.—Growth of roots, stems, and leaves.—Form as dependent on growth.—Movements dependent on growth.—Movements of protoplasm.—Turgescence.—Circumnutation of roots, stems, leaves.—Seedling plants.

In considering the growth of plants we have to distinguish that growth which is mere extension of old material from that which is the result of the formation of new substance. We have an illustration of the first case in the earliest stages of germination of a seed, or in the sprouting of a potato in a cellar. Growth may and does take place in such instances without any real increase of substance, or any augmented weight save what may be derived from water. The plant in this stage lives upon the resources stored up in its tissues, and will continue to do so until they are exhausted. But growth, in the sense of real increase of substance or of increased weight from the addition of new material, depends upon the amount of carbon assimilated, as already referred to under the heading of leaves. A plant with leaf-green or chlorophyll in its tissues (and it is with these alone that we are here concerned) gains carbon in the form of carbonic acid gas when it is exposed to light, and loses it constantly, whether in light or darkness. Nevertheless, as the total gain is greater than the loss, the balance is in favor of the plant. The plant may thus be considered to be the result of the greater amount of work done (under the influence of sunlight) through the medium of the green cells than of that accomplished by the colorless cells, even though their action is continuous, and that of the green cells intermittent. It is for us now to enquire how this increase of substance, how this growth and building up of new materials takes place. The circumstances that are propitious, or which are antagonistic to it, have been considered; it remains to enquire into the way in which the process itself is effected, and, for this purpose, we must revert to the fabric of the plant, and go back to the cell.

Growth of Cells.—The perfect cell, as has been explained, consists of a membranous bag enclosing the protoplasm, some liquid contents, and in the growing state a small, highly refracting oval body known as the "nucleus." The growth of a cell may take place in one of three different ways. There may be simple extension of the cell membrane, which becomes stretched by the influx of fluid into its cavity, producing a state of "turgescence" in the cell. But this turgescence, which is of intermittent occurrence, is of itself hardly to be truly considered as growth in the sense of the formation of new material, although so closely associated with it that no true growth can take place without it.

A second mode of growth, resulting in the real addition of material, and consequent increase of weight, is that called "intercalary," because new material is supposed to be intercalated or squeezed in between the old. Thus, the molecules of cell-membrane are separated by the pressure caused by the turgid protoplasm, and into the interstices so formed, new molecules of membrane formed by the protoplasm are, as it were, squeezed. The process is as if a number of grains of sand were laid upon a table, each grain just touching its neighbor, and then a new grain were forced in between two others, only in this case the new grain is formed in the cell itself. The requisite pressure is afforded, in the case of the cell, by the growing protoplasm within, and by the influx of fluid into the cell by osmosis, producing a condition of turgescence. The growth of the protoplasm itself takes place precisely in the same way as that of the cell membrane—viz., by the formation of new particles, which are squeezed in by intercalary growth between the older ones. New matter is also deposited on the outer surface of the protoplasm or inner surface of the cell wall.

Lastly, growth is effected, not merely by extension of old cells, or by incorporation of new materials with old, but by actual increase in the number of cells. This increase in number has been brought about by the subdivision of the protoplasm into two or more segments, each of which becomes invested by cell-membrane.

For full details as to the various ways in which division of the protoplasm and the formation of new cells take place, reference must be made to text books. What has been here said is sufficient to indicate the general nature of growth in the organs—with which we are here most concerned—the root, the stem, and the leaf.

Growing Points.—As has been stated, all the parts of plants are at first wholly cellular and structurally indistinguishable; but, as growth goes on, not only their outer form alters, but the form and arrangement of their constituent cells also, so that various tissues—fibrous, woody, vascular, or epidermal—are formed; and thus it comes about that in the fully developed root the internal structure and the arrangement of the tissues are different in the great majority of cases from those of the stem, those of the stem from those of the leaf, and so on—different, that is to say, in so far as the arrangement of the elementary cells and tissues go, rather than as far as the cells themselves and their modifications are concerned. But while there is this difference in the structure of the adult leaf, stem, and root respectively, all the time these organs retain their active faculty of growth there remains a portion of the cellular tissue in its original unmodified condition—the cells ready to divide and multiply and so bring about the growth of the organ. This portion is called the "cambium" or "meristem." So far as growth in length is concerned, there are certain special points where subdivision of cells is most active. These are called the "growing points." At these places the cells divide rapidly, each cell remaining small, and not, as elsewhere, greatly extending its size by interstitial growth.

Growth of Roots.—The growing point of a root, so far as its length is concerned, is comprised within a small area just above the extreme tip, the extreme tip itself being, as previously stated, covered by a little cap shed off from the skin of the root and serving as a shield to it in its progress through the soil.

That the growth in length takes place over a very small area adjacent to the tip of the root is proved by a very simple observation. If marks be made on the growing root at equal distances apart, say one-eighth inch, and the progress of growth be watched from day to day, then it will be found that while the uppermost marks remain equi-distant, those near the tip become more or less widely separated. This experiment is easily carried out with a hyacinth growing in a glass vase, or by allowing a bean to germinate on the surface of wet moss. It will thus also be seen that the actual area in which growth in length is going on is very small, and that its greatest activity is not exactly at the extreme point, but a little above it, between it and the point where the root-hairs begin to emerge. There is, then, in the growing root—first, at the extreme tip a root-cap or shield, constantly renewed from within by the growth of the cells above or within it; then a region of very limited extent, devoted to the growth in length of the root; and above that a portion, usually but not always, provided with root-hairs, and which is especially told off to fulfil the duties of absorption.

As the upper, thicker part of the root is relatively fixed, it will be seen how the fine root fibrils are, by the situation of their growing point, enabled to push their way, by constant renewal at their growing point, in amongst the particles of the soil when the conditions are favorable.

Growth of the Stem.—In the case of the stem and branches, the growing points, by whose agency increase in length takes place, are placed at the summit of the stem or of its subdivisions, the branches. The growing points then form the substance of the "buds," which are either invested by leaf-scales as protectors and stores of nourishment, as in the case of bulb-scales, or by perfect leaves. The increase in the thickness of stems takes place also by means of the growing tissue or cambium, the situation of which is different in the two main groups of "Exogens" and "Endogens."

To the former series belong all our trees and shrubs, the clovers, beet-roots, turnips, and the vast majority of plants which have the veins of their leaves disposed in a network. In these plants the woody bundles of which the stem is principally made up consist of "wood cells" and "bast cells," with vessels of various kinds; and on the outer side of each bundle is a thin layer of cambium tissue capable of growth, and in virtue of which the woody bundles increase on their outer surface. These woody bundles accumulate in wedge-like masses, and these again are arranged in concentric rings around the central cellular pith, thus forming the rings visible on the cut surface of the trunk of a tree, one such ring generally indicating, in these latitudes, the growth of one season, or at least of one growing period.

In Endogens, to which all the cereals, and the grasses and almost all plants in which the veins of the leaf run parallel or nearly so, the woody bundles have their cambium tissue in the centre of each bundle, so that their growth in diameter is limited by the pressure of the older tissues outside, and there are no concentric rings in the stem. Indeed, in this country, such plants do not produce a woody stem.

Growth of Leaves.—The growing points of leaves occur in various situations, according to the kind of leaf. Sometimes and more generally the direction of principal growth is from within outward—that is to say, from the centre outward (centrifugal); in other cases, the general tendency is in the opposite direction (centripetal). In addition to these growing points at definite spots, where new cells are always forming during the active period, new growth may occur in isolated spots by the formation of growing cells in the midst of or between others that have lost their faculty of growth, and thus growth in the substance of the plant may take place by intercalation as well as at the extremities.

To repeat, then, true growth consists in the formation of new protoplasm from the old, and in the division of the protoplasm into new cells. This division takes place especially and primarily, so far as growth in length is concerned, at certain definite places called growing points. The new tissues thus formed are at first wholly cellular, some of the constituent cells retaining the faculty of sub-division, though sometimes not manifesting it till a later period ; while others become modified in various ways as growth goes on, forming wood-cells, fibres, epidermis, and so on.

Form as Dependent on Growth.—If we could suppose the degree or intensity of growth to be equal on all sides, and without impediment or obstacle, the result would be a spherical plant ; and such plants do exist, but, in the great majority of cases, the conditions are such that growth is greater in amount in one direction than in another ; or it may be that while part remains stationary another part grows, the result being a change of form. In the case of the main root and stem, the principal direction of growth is vertically upwards and downwards ; in the case of leaves, the main direction of growth is horizontal, so that while a stem or a root may be divided from above downwards into two nearly equal halves, one half the reflex of the other, a leaf must be divided horizontally, and the upper surface and the lower surface are commonly different. Variations in form are dependent not only on variations in the direction of growth, but upon the place where growth is taking place, and whether it be limited, as in the case of the growing points and cambium tissue already referred to, or general throughout the mass.

The form of the plant or of any particular part of it will also of necessity vary according as the growth is continuous or intermittent, equal or unequal. These are all circumstances readily understood, and they are referred to here because they furnish the reasons for the development of bulb and root, as of turnip and mangel as contrasted with that of foliage. In them also must be sought the explanation of thin ears of wheat or defective hay crops.

Phenomena associated with Growth and Activity.—Under this heading may be mentioned the various movements in the liquid (cell-sap), contained within the cells, and in the protoplasm, which are observed in living cells, especially in those in which the vital processes are most active. Here also may be mentioned the movements associated more or less directly with growth, and the influence of various agencies, such as of gravitation, light, temperature, etc., on plants and their several organs. These phenomena and these influences are more manifest during active growth; and when they occur in living organs which have ceased their actual growth, they do not essentially differ, though they may do so in degree, and may also, to some extent, be modified in character.

Movements as Dependent on Growth.—But a few years ago the notion of movement taking place in plants, other than that produced by the wind or other mechanical agency, was, if not entirely ignored, so little considered that the immobility of plants was contrasted with the mobility of animals. We know now that even locomotion is by no means an exclusive attribute of animals, but for our present purposes we need only refer to those movements more immediately connected with the growth.

Movement of Protoplasm.—The protoplasm is a very mobile substance, and the cell-membrane is very elastic, while both, as has been shown, are permeable in various degrees by water, the consequence of which is that under favorable conditions the cells become turgid. As the degree of turgescence varies according to circumstances, tension being followed by flaccidity, and flaccidity overcome by turgidity, is of course obvious not only that changes of form must ensue from these differences in the degree of tension of the cells, but that movements of the parts concerned must also take place. These movements are, of course, more obvious when growth is irregular and unequal. Turgescence of the cells, as has been said, is an essential condition of growth, and if this turgescence take place on one side of a stem, or on one surface of a leaf only, a curve will be produced, the convexity of which will be along the line of greatest swelling and growth—the concavity on the opposite side where growth is less active, or altogether inoperative. The rapidly growing upper surface will be restrained as by a bridle by that part which is growing more slowly or not at all, and hence the curvature.

Circumnutation.—Now, let us suppose the very frequent case where the greatest intensity of growth is now in one place, now in another, then, of course, we should have the curvatures first in one place, and then in another, and this is what happens in the case of growing shoots whose tips gradually revolve, forming circuits or ellipses of greater or less extent with greater or less rapidity, according to circumstances. This movement, which is not usually perceptible except by the use of delicate instruments, may sometimes be watched by the naked eye, even in the case of such apparently stiff parts as the leading shoots of Firs. Among other objects gained by this movement of "revolving nutation," or as Darwin called it, "circumnutation," is the exposure of each leaf in turn to the conditions of light most favorable to it.

Movement of the Tip of the Root.—While the elongation of the root near the tip takes place in the manner described, the force of growth is not equal throughout the whole region at the same time. Supposing the fibril to be made up of cells piled up one upon another in longitudinal rows, then the greatest energy of growth, marked by the turgescence of the cells, occurs at one time in one row, to shift at another time into the next row, and so on in succession all round the root. The effect of this greater turgescence and intensity of growth—now in one place, now at another—is to move the tip of the root, not in a circle, because growth is going on behind the tip as it moves, but in an advancing spiral coil, so that the tip is forced to enter the soil and to penetrate between its particles, just as the point of a corkscrew is made by the pressure of the hand to penetrate the cork, the pressure of the hand being replaced, in the case of the root, by the superincumbent weight of soil.

Darwin, who has done so much to illustrate and make known the movements of roots and of other organs, calculates that the terminal growing part of the radicle (or primary root produced from the seedling plant) "increases in length with a force equal to . . . the pressure of at least a quarter of a pound—probably with a much greater force when prevented from bending to any side by the surrounding earth. While thus increasing in length, it increases in thickness, pushing away the damp earth on all sides with a force of above eight pounds in one case, of three pounds in another case. . . . The growing part, therefore, does not act like a nail when hammered into a board, but more like a wedge of wood, which, whilst slowly driven into a crevice, continually expands at the same time by the absorption of water; and a wedge thus acting will split even a mass of rock."

Movement of Stems.—The circumnutation of stems as a result, or at least as a concomitant of active growth, is most easily seen in the case of climbing plants like the hop, the free ends of whose growing shoots sweep round in wide curves till they come in contact with a support round which to twine,* and thus remove their leaves from the surface, where they would be overshadowed, to a point of vantage where they would be exposed to light, and this with the least expenditure of material. Very similar are the movements executed by stolons and runners, as of the strawberry, and probably, though the cases have not been studied, of the trailing rhizomes of the twitch (*Triticum repens*), the scions of the meadow poa (*Poa pratensis*), of the clovers, of the milfoil, etc. Such a movement would facilitate the introduction of these runners between other plants, and thus secure the extension of their area of growth. The movements in the stem are more especially connected with growth; they cease, or become much enfeebled after growth is completed or arrested. Under certain circumstances, however, the faculty of growth is retained in certain spots after it has ceased elsewhere, or if actual growth do not take place, yet some of the phenomena connected with it may occur. Thus the stems of grasses, such as of wheat, are provided with thick "nodes" or joints at the places whence the leaves spring from the stem. When the wheat gets beaten down or laid by a storm of rain and wind, the resumption of the erect position is effected by the medium of the nodes, which grow, or at least become turgescent, especially on the under surface, which thus becomes convex, while the upper surface, which does not grow, or at least not to the same extent, becomes concave; the consequence is that the upper end of the stem becomes raised—as may be illustrated thus :—Let——— represent the joint of the laid stem ; then, by the agencies just mentioned, the straight horizontal position is replaced by the ascending one /, and ultimately by the vertical one |

---

* See Darwin, *The Movements and Habits of Climbing Plants.*

Darwin has shown that the joints of grass stems continue to exhibit movements on a small scale for a long period. Supposing the stem to be "laid," such movements would clearly aid the upward tendency above described, and facilitate the uprising of the stem. (Darwin, *Power of Movement*, p. 503).

Movements of Leaves.—The leaves of plants exhibit several kinds of motion; some periodic, as in the case of the so-called sleep of leaves, some due to the stimulus of light or its removal, some the consequence of contact, as in the case of the sensitive plant; but those to which mention is here made are the result of the same causes as those before alluded to in the case of stems and roots. The growth movements of leaves are observable in the stalk, or in the blade, or in both, and are chiefly exerted in a vertical direction, so that the leaf rises or falls; but as the ascent is never quite in the same line as the descent, some side to side motion must also take place. It is noticed that the rise occurs generally in the evening, the fall on the following morning. These movements are probably due to the intensity of growth being greater first on one side, then on the other.

Growth-movements of the kind indicated have now been shown to exist in the roots, in the stems, and in the leaves. The probability is that they occur more or less wherever growth is going on actively. In accordance with this, it may be mentioned that seedling plants manifest these movements to a remarkable degree. Thus all the parts of seedling cabbages, the radicle, the caulicle above the radicle supporting the seed leaves or cotyledons, as well as these latter organs, were observed by Darwin to exhibit growth movements facilitating the downward passage of the root and the upward progress of the caulicles.

CHAPTER IV.

SENSITIVENESS.

Movements dependent on external conditions. — Gravitation, light, heat, moisture.—Action of gravity on roots.—Geotropism.—Influence of light, heat, moisture, and contact on roots.—Passage of roots through the soil.—Action of gravitation on leaves.—Heliotropism.—Sleep of leaves.—Action of heat and moisture on leaves.—Defensive arrangements.—Selection of hardy varieties.—Influence of contact on leaves.—Action of gravity, light, heat, moisture, and contact on stems. — After-effects. — Climbing plants.— Combined effect of external and internal agencies.

Closely analogous to the growth-movements are a series of alterations of position dependent upon various circumstances, such as gravity, the influence of heat and light or their absence, the result of contact or irritation, and so on. They are probably essentially of the same nature as the growth movements, but, unlike them, they are not confined to structures still in a growing state; moreover, in some cases they exhibit a sort of reflex action, contact or irritation of one part bringing about a movement of some other part at a distance. It is often difficult to dissociate the effects of these several movements; for a living plant and its parts are subjected at the same time to the combined influence of several of these agencies, and the force and direction of growth are necessarily essentially modified by them.

It may be well in this place to indicate very generally in what manner roots, stems, and leaves are sensitive to the effects of gravity, light, moisture, and actual contact or irritation, and then to specify equally briefly what is the general character of the results produced by these several causes acting singly, or in combination.

The Action of Gravity on Roots.—Geotropism.—The downward tendency of the main root is one of its most marked characteristics, and this tendency to grow, or move towards the centre of the earth under the influence of gravitation, is known as "geotropism," the opposite tendency being called "apogeotropism." Knight was the first to show that downward tendencies of the root were due to gravitation, and this he did by causing seedlings to grow on a wheel kept in motion. The effect of gravity was here overcome by the movement of the wheel, and the rootlets, instead of growing downwards, were now directed away from the centre of the wheel. Darwin shows (*l. c.*, p. 540) that it is the tip of the root alone that is involved in this downward tendency, the destruction of the tip putting a stop to the movement. While the primary root or radicle under favorable circumstances penetrates the soil perpendicularly downwards, the secondary ones bend obliquely, not perpendicularly, downwards, the tertiary ramifications and their subdivisions being so little affected by geotropism that they grow out freely in all directions. From this manner of growth in the main root and its branches respectively, it is evident how the whole mass of soil within their reach becomes, under favorable conditions, a happy hunting ground for the roots. Moreover, it has been shown that where the primary radicle, the origin of the "tap" root, has been destroyed—as it often must be in nature, by insects or other means—the secondary roots, instead of retaining their oblique direction, assume that previously taken by the injured root and pass downwards.

The Action of Light and Heat on Roots.—The direct action of light upon ordinary roots is, of course, usually of a negative character. The form and direction of growth in the root may, however, be affected by differences of temperature, experienced now on one side, now on another. Darwin has shown that the movements of roots, due to irritation or contact, are checked by too high or too low a temperature. During their passage through the soil, the roots must be constantly subjected to variations of temperature, first on one side and then on another, these variations giving rise to some of the curvatures and bends of the rootlets. The effect of an excessive amount of heat in the soil upon the germination of seedlings has been studied by M. Prillieux, and is of interest as indicating the conditions under which tuberous roots and root stocks may, under certain circumstances, be formed. When seedlings of French beans and vegetable marrows were grown in an overheated soil, the caulicle or portion of the stem above the root and between it and the seed-leaves became preternaturally swollen and tuberous, while growth in hight was arrested. The increased development arising from the heated soil took place, therefore, in the very same organs which constitute the so-called "bulbs" of turnips or "roots" of swedes or mangels. The increased volume is due principally to an excessive development of existing cells rather than to a multiplication of new ones.

The Action of Moisture on Roots.—Much more obvious to the general observer is the action of moisture on roots. The distance to which roots will travel in search as it were of water, and the way in which luxuriant growth and intricate ramification are promoted, when access to it is obtained, are familiar facts. Too frequently drain pipes get choked with a mass of roots whose structure has been changed, and whose excessive growth has been stimulated by the presence of copious supplies of moisture. If there is an equal supply of water all round, the growth of the roots will be uniform; but if, as is more often the case, there is more water on one side than on the other, then the root will curve to the side where there is the fullest supply, and the power thus exerted to get at the water is greater than that of gravity.

When the tip of the root is covered with grease, the root does not bend to the wet surface, on which account Mr. Darwin and his son infer that sensitiveness to moisture resides specially in the tip. The relation these movements and this growth bear to the processes of nutrition carried on by the roots is too obvious to need further comment.

The Influence of Contact on Roots.—The effect of pressure such as that caused by the contact of any substance, even if it be very slight, is to produce movements of curvature in the root, the direction of the curvature varying according to the part of the root touched. Thus, if the root be touched in the region where growth is going on most actively, the root becomes concave on the side which is touched, convex on the opposite side, probably because growth is arrested by the pressure on the one side, while it is unrestricted on the other. The consequence of this is that the roots in such case turn towards the obstructing substance, and, if it be of small dimensions, coil themselves around it, or, if it be too large for this purpose, creep over its surface.

On the other hand, if the extreme tip of the root be touched, the root bends away from the obstruction, becoming convex on the side where contact is effected, concave on the opposite side, the root sometimes making complete loops by its continued curved growth. The object of this sensibility to contact appears to be to enable the roots to overcome the obstacles they meet with in the soil. Thus "when a root meets with an obstacle in its way, the pressure on one side of the tip causes the growing part of the root to grow more rapidly on the side of the obstacle, and thus curve away from it" (F. Darwin).

It will be seen that the irritation from the various causes above mentioned is not merely local in its effect, but that it induces movement in adjoining parts, on which account the parts so influenced are spoken of as "sensitive."

Passage of Roots through the Soil—Summary.—The course followed by a root through the soil is, says Darwin, "brought about and modified by extraordinarily complex and diversified agencies—by geotropism, acting, as has just been explained, in a different manner on the primary, secondary, and tertiary radicles; by sensitiveness to contact, different in kind in the apex and in the part immediately above the apex; and apparently by sensitiveness to the varying dampness of different parts of the soil. . . . The direction which the apex takes at each successive period of the growth of a root ultimately determines its whole course; it is, therefore, highly important that the apex should pursue from the first the most advantageous direction; and we can thus understand why sensitiveness to gravitation, to contact, and to moisture, all reside in the tip, and why the tip determines the upper growing part to bend either to or from the exciting cause. A radicle may be compared with a burrowing animal, such as a mole, which wishes to penetrate perpendicularly down into the ground. By continually moving his head from side to side, or circumnutating, he feels any stone or other obstacle, as well as any difference in the hardness of the soil, and he will turn from that side. If the earth is damper on one than on the other side, he will turn thither as to better hunting ground. Nevertheless, after each interruption, guided by the sense of gravity, he will be able to recover his downward course and to burrow to a greater depth."

Elsewhere Darwin sums up the root movements as follows:—"We believe that there is no structure in plants more wonderful, so far as its functions are concerned, than the tip of the radicle. If the tip be lightly pressed, or burnt or cut, it transmits an influence to the upper adjoining part, causing it to bend away from the affected side; and, what is more surprising, the tip can distinguish between a slightly harder and softer object by which it is simultaneously pressed on opposite sides. If, however, the radicle is pressed by a similar object above the tip, the pressed part does not transmit any influence to the more distant parts, but bends abruptly towards the object. If the tip perceives the air to be moister on one side than on the other, it likewise transmits an influence to the upper adjoining part, which bends towards the source of moisture. When the tip is excited by light, the adjoining part bends from the light; but when excited by gravitation, the same part tends towards the centre of gravity. In almost every case we can clearly perceive the final purpose or advantage of the several movements. Two or perhaps more of the exciting causes often act simultaneously on the tip, and one conquers the other, no doubt, in accordance with its importance for the life of the plant. The course pursued by the radicle in penetrating the ground must be determined by the tip; hence it has acquired such diverse kinds of sensitiveness. It is hardly an exaggeration to say that the tip of the radicle thus endowed, and having the power of directing the movements of the adjoining parts, acts like the brain of one of the lower animals, the brain being seated within the anterior end of the body, receiving impressions from the sense-organs, and directing the several movements."

Practical Inferences.—It will be obvious, then, from what has been before said, that for cultural purposes, such as the various operations connected with tillage, the nature, quantity, and time of application of manure, and the like, the character of root-action in general must be studied in connection with the nature and properties of the soil. The special form and characteristics of the root in the particular crop it is wished to cultivate—tap-rooted, fibrous-rooted, fleshy, surface-rooting, or deep-rooting, etc.—must also be taken into consideration in the same relation.

Action of Gravitation on Leaves.—The tendency of leaves during their growing period so to place themselves that their upper surface looks to the heaven, their lower to the earth, is a matter of every-day observation. Scarcely less familiar are the turns and twists which the leaves or their stalks make to right themselves when by any means their normal position is interfered with. At first sight it would seem that these movements must be due rather to the influence of light than of gravitation; but as they take place in darkness as well as in light, and as they do not take place when plants are so grown as to be exempt from the influence of gravitation, it is clear what the true cause of these movements is (Van Tieghem).

Action of Light on Leaves — Heliotropism. — The chemical changes which result from the exposure of the leaves to light have already been alluded to under the head of nutrition. It remains here to mention the power that they have of turning to the light, now called "heliotropism," and especially of so placing their upper surface as that it shall form a right angle to the direction of the light. It had been surmised that the horizontal position of leaves, and especially the position with regard to the direction of light, was due to the conjoint action of gravitation of geotropism, of heliotropism, and of the greater relative force of growth on one or the other surface. The particular direction assumed by the leaves was supposed to be due to the balance between these forces; but by means of experiments made with a view of annulling or counteracting the effects of gravitation, and of unequal growth, Mr. Francis Darwin has shown that the power which leaves have of placing themselves at right angles to incident light is due to a special sensitiveness. This sensitiveness is capable of regulating the action of other forces, whether external to the plant, as that of gravitation, or internal, such as that controlling the direction and amount of growth. The movements of the leaves towards the light are different from others which are of a periodic character, in that they are influenced by the direction rather than by the intensity of the light.

The growth of leaves, like growth in general, is retarded by the action of light. Growth, therefore, is carried on independently of and not contemporaneously with nutrition by the leaf, so far as the latter consists in the decomposition of carbonic acid and the fixation of the carbon. Thus it has been shown by Dr. Vines that leaves will grow in darkness, or under the influence of blue light; in air deprived of carbonic acid; and even in the absence of chlorophyll. But although there is thus shown to be no direct relation between nutrition and growth, yet there is, of course, an indirect relation; growth under the apparently adverse conditions just mentioned, being only possible in cases where there is available some store of nourishment previously formed by assimilation.

Sleep of Leaves.—Other movements of leaves are dependent chiefly on the amount of light to which they are subjected. Of such nature are the movements popularly supposed to be connected with the sleep of plants, but which have no real analogy with the sleep of animals. Clover and sainfoin leaves show these nocturnal movements very clearly, the leaflets folding up at the approach of night, and unfolding in the morning as the light increases. Plants exposed to the dark end of the solar spectrum manifest similar movements. Some leaves are raised, others depressed, some fold upwards, some downwards, but the object in all cases is probably the same—namely, to shield the leaves from the cooling effect of radiation from the surface during the night, a process which produces the same effects as actual frost would do. The cause of these movements is due to a swelling or turgescence and a consequent growth first on one side and then on another side.

Action of Heat and Moisture upon Leaves.—But little beyond what has already been mentioned need be said upon the relation of heat and moisture to leaves. A few words upon the influence of excessive temperatures may, however, here be appropriately given.

If the temperature fall below a given point, variable for each species, and also for each individual plant, the functions of the leaf are held in abeyance, chlorophyll is only imperfectly formed (hence the yellow tinge of frosted wheat); and if the temperature be still further depressed death results.

Action of Frost.—When a leaf is frozen the fluid contents escape from the cells by permeation through their membrane, and freeze on the outside of the cell, so that the spaces between them are full of ice. It rarely happens that the juices of the cells freeze in the interior of the cells—if they do, rupture of the cell wall and death are the most probable results. Under ordinary circumstances the cells lose that turgescence which, as has been stated, is necessary for their activity. All the functions of life are arrested, not necessarily never to be resumed, for, in some cases, when the ice in the tissues of the plant melts, the water is re-absorbed by the membrane, and life action is resumed. Winter wheat must frequently become frozen in this manner, but it is comparatively rarely that the plant is killed outright, farmers wisely choosing those varieties which experience has shown to be the hardiest. If the cold is sufficient to kill the leaves or any portion of them, the leaves become limp and blackened. The limpness is easily accounted for by the causes we have mentioned, as well as by the stoppage of supplies of water from the root. The discoloration is the effect of some molecular change in the chlorophyll at present not understood.

Action of Excessive Heat.—Too high a temperature also arrests or perverts all the functions of the leaf. Where transpiration is excessive, and the absorption of fresh supplies not in proportion, the leaves speedily wither, as may be seen in a field of mangels on a hot day, when the evaporation of watery vapor from the surface is greater than the absorption of moisture by the root. On the other hand, during the night, while the roots are still at work, the transpiring power of the leaf is lessened, and drops of water exude from the leaves. Where the temperature is so high as to kill the plant or leaf outright, it is the protoplasm which dies; its constitution and molecular construction become changed, its power of absorbing water destroyed, and thus the turgid condition of the cells is lost.

Defensive Arrangements.—Prejudicial effects, either of a too low or a too high temperature, are moderated by the conformation of the leaf, the thickness of its skin, the arrangement of its tissues, the presence of hairs, and other structural endowments. These circumstances render the selection of the particular variety most suitable for any special locality a matter of the greatest moment. In the case of wheat, for instance, some varieties are much more tender than others. Bearded wheats are as a rule hardier than the beardless ones. A variety known as the Blood Red is very hardy, owing its immunity possibly to its habit of keeping its leaves close to the ground during the winter and spring, and, therefore, less exposed to sudden changes of temperature. In any case, its leaves are more likely to be protected by a coating of snow. The selection, therefore, of the kind of wheat best adapted for Scotland, for the eastern or for the western counties of England respectively, is a matter of great consequence. A variety which succeeds in a warm moist climate would be quite unsuitable for a drier one, even if the temperature sometimes rose higher.

In moist air it has lately been shown by M. Vesque that the leaves are both thinner and longer than when grown in dry air, that the vascular bundles of the stem are also thinner, and less perfectly developed than in dry air. Thus, the effects of a saturated atmosphere on the growth of leaves seem to be very similar to those mentioned by Rauwenhof as characteristic of plants grown in obscurity. When fully exposed to the light, in a dry, hot, stagnant atmosphere, where transpiration from the surface of leaves is ample, the leaves become thicker, their anatomical structure is altered, and they show a tendency to become more hairy.

It would not be worth while for the agriculturist to try and make his plants adapt themselves to different conditions as the experimentalists and physiologists do, but the indications and facts brought forward by the latter may very profitably influence the farmer's selection of the particular varieties best suited, by their conformation or structure, to meet the vicissitudes of particular localities.

The Influence of Contact on Leaves.—This may be dismissed with a few words only, as it is not, so far as at present known, of much practical importance to agriculturists. In addition to the movements immediately connected with growth, gravitation, or the action of light, which are manifested only during active growth, there are others which occur in the fully-developed leaf, as the periodical night and day movements, the movements affected by light and temperature, and lastly, those which are caused by mechanical contact, as by the impact of certain nitrogenous substances, as in the so-called carnivorous leaves before referred to, and those caused by a touch or other mechanical effect, as in the leaves of the sensitive plant. Chloroform and ether arrest these movements, while they have no effect upon the movements that are due to light and heat. The cause of the movements in question is attributed to the sudden contraction of the protoplasm, the expulsion of the watery contents of the cells forming the lower portion of the swelling which leaves endowed with this property possess at the base of their stalks. The cells so emptied become flaccid, and the leaf in consequence falls. The water expelled from the interior of the cells passes into the spaces between them and into the stem, as in the case of frozen leaves (p. 65), and is re-absorbed when the irritation ceases. The balance being restored, the leaf resumes its horizontal position.

The Action of Gravity on Stems.—The cause of the upward growth of stems, though so familiar, is not understood. It is in general exerted in opposition to the direction of gravitation. If a stem be bent downwards, growth takes place much more rapidly on the lower surface, tending to make it convex on the lower surface, and consequently to raise its free end (see p. 54). It is this tendency, which, as has been previously stated, permits the stalks of the wheat when laid to recover their erect position. Some stem or portions of stem are, however, directly influenced by gravitation, as in the case of underground stems and branches, which burrow in the ground to produce tubers; and it is clear, from the position and direction of the branches of a tree, that the influence of gravity, direct or negative, varies greatly in different cases, so that on the whole it is probable that the directions in question are more especially due to varying degrees of intensity of growth in different situations, according to local necessities and the action of light, than to gravitation pure and simple.

Influence of Light on Stems. — The remarks made under the corresponding heading in regard to leaves, apply with the necessary modifications to stems. The stems have often a marked tendency to move or grow towards the light, but the opposite tendency is shown in other instances, as in the ivy, the runners of the strawberry, and other cases, where this peculiarity favors the application of the stem to the surface of the ground, of a wall, or of any means of support, as in many climbing plants.

The action of light in retarding growth, already referred to, seems opposed to many of the phenomena just recorded — such as the bending of the stems towards the light, the fact that stems grow by day as well as by night, the circumstance that the tissues of plants grown in the dark are feeble and ill-developed. These apparent contradictions may be explained by the fact that the retarding influence of growth, which is so manifest when the plant is grown under artificial conditions, when the influence of other agencies is prevented or excluded, is compensated for or overcome by other agencies — temperature, moisture, etc. — when the plant is grown under natural conditions. Again, what is called the "after effect" has to be considered — the facilities for growth afforded by the absence of light, by the agency of heat, or other forces, may continue after those influences have ceased to act, and so a plant may grow for a time under adverse influences by reason of the impetus gained when circumstances were more favorable.

Influence of Heat and Moisture on the Stem.—The growth of the stem is directly influenced by heat, there being in this as in other cases a minimum below which growth cannot take place, an optimum at which it takes place most vigorously, and a maximum beyond which heat is injurious. The favorable influence of heat it is which in part overcomes the influence of gravitation, and enables the stem to ascend. The stem will grow fastest and strongest on the side most exposed to the heat, if that heat be not excessive, and this tendency will remove it from the soil. Similarly a moist condition of the atmosphere favors growth, and the stem will grow the faster on the side most exposed to the moist vapor, and, owing to the convexity so formed, it will in consequence bend its free end and its concavity towards the drier side.

Influence of Contact on Stems—Climbing Plants.—The most marked instance of this occurs in the case of climbing plants. We have already seen that the young growing parts of plants very generally exhibit gyratory movements, these movements being produced by inequalities of growth, now in this direction, now in that, the result being that the free end moves round, and that these movements are only indirectly affected by temperature or light. In the case of climbing plants, such as the hop, the dodder, the tendrils of the pea or of the vine, which are peculiarly sensitive to contact, these movements are much more marked, the object being to secure a suitable means of attachment, and so to expose the leaves when present to the influence of light and air with the least expenditure of force and tissue. Such plants, in fact, depend upon others for their mechanical support. When the free end of such a plant or a tendril comes into contact with the straw of a wheat plant, growth is checked on the surface by which contact is made, while it is increased on the opposite side. As a consequence, one side of the climber is flattened against the supporting plant, while the other side, growing more rapidly, becomes convex, and its tip is forced in process of growth round the supporting stem. The increased growth on the convex side of the coil is thus the direct outcome of the impression produced by contact.

Combined Effect of the Preceding Causes. — The effects of light, heat, gravitation, etc., on growing plants are thus seen to be manifold, and when considered separately seem often conflicting and contrary to common experience. The reason is that under natural conditions the one influence counteracts the other, the growth of the plant being the outcome of the combined effect of all the causes alluded to, and of the operation at one time, and under one set of circumstances, of the influence of one agency (controlled or not by others), at another time of a different agency. This affords an explanation of the fact that the seasons marked by extraordinary productiveness are not those wherein some one or more of the conditions have been specially favorable at a particular time, even though that time be the growing period, but those in which the conditions have been generally propitious throughout. The physiologist endeavors to isolate the agencies which influence growth in order to ascertain precisely what each does independently of the others; the practical man has to deal with the combined effect of all, but it is clear that the combination cannot be properly understood unless the separate effect of each component be first clearly comprehended.

CHAPTER V.

DEVELOPMENT.

Progressive changes during growth.—Morphological, physical, and physiological.— Influence of inheritance.—Variation.— Selection.—Reserve-materials: their formation and transport. — Germination. — Maturation.—Ripening of fruits and seeds.

Development as here understood includes those progressive changes of form and appearance which accompany the growth of a plant from an infantile to an adult state. It forms no part of our present plan to pursue this part of the subject here, as any elementary text-book contains sufficient details as to the progressive organization of flowering plants. Growth considered separately results in increase of bulk only, but development includes the whole cycle of changes which convert an atom of homogeneous protoplasm into a tree laden with fruit or into a wheat plant heavy with golden ears. A mangel or a turnip which, under favorable circumstances, gets bigger and bigger, may be said to grow. It increases in size and weight, but neither its outward appearance nor its internal construction is otherwise much affected. The giant mangels exhibited at root shows illustrate growth rather than development. They are very big, but their nutritive power is by no means in proportion to their size, as the quantity of nutritive matter developed is small indeed as compared with the great quantity of water they contain. Growth, in fact, is but the preparatory stage, during which material and machinery are acquired, to be turned to subsequent use in the consolidation of the stem, the construction of flower and seed, the formation and storage of reserve food-materials, of starch, of oil, of the various secretions, such as the caoutchouc, the alkaloids, as quinine, morphia, and many others.

Growth and development may go on together at the same time, as we see in an oak tree, which puts forth its midsummer shoots at the same time that it is ripening its acorns and consolidating the new wood; but in an herbaceous plant, like the wheat, as development proceeds growth ceases—at least, to a great extent. So in the case of such plants as the turnip, the mangel, and the hop, when the plant commences to enter upon the flowering stage, then changes—not merely of bulk, but of outward form, and to some extent of inward construction and chemical composition—occur. So, as the soft tissues harden into solid wood by deposit of woody matter in their wood cells, development takes place; and, as the water and the salts taken up by the roots and the gases inspired by the leaves act and re-act upon one another—aided or not, as the case may be, by the agency of light—various changes occur which may be included under the head of development. Development, then, is morphological in so far as it relates to the conformation of the plant, chemical or physical—in so far as it includes the chemical and physical changes which accompany the passage from the young to the old, from the crude and imperfect to the complete and mature. The conditions which favor development in the sense here understood are thus more or less opposite to those which foster growth. Gardeners recognize this by affording plenty of water and sufficient heat to their plants when growing, and by reducing the amount of water as the plant is about to produce flower, fruit, and seed. They apply liquid manure in the growing stage, but withhold it in the ripening period. They root-prune their fruit trees when growth is too vigorous and fruit production too scanty. They check rampant growth by keeping the roots in small-sized pots. The farmer unfortunately has not the same control over his plants that the gardener has, but he is careful as to the time when he applies manure. He is not particularly distressed at a wet growing season, but he looks forward with hope to a relatively dry, hot period for the corn to ripen. Of great practical importance also is it to note the different effects of manures as particularly observed at Rothamsted; some, such as nitrogenous manures, stimulating growth more especially; others, such as the alkalis and superphosphates, being more particularly favorable to the ripening of the seed or the consolidation of the straw by the formation of woody fibre.

Growth is the same throughout all plants, but the mode of development is much more specialized. In its initial stages, the atom of protoplasm that is to be the future potato plant, is not appreciably different from that which is destined to grow into a wheat plant or into a fruit tree. While growth is common to all plants and uniform in character, development is special and different, less or more, in the case of each particular species or kind of plant. Outward conditions greatly influence the amount of growth, while they have relatively less influence on the extent, still less on the direction of development in the individual plant.

Inheritance.—A particular kind of plant, therefore, may retain its characteristics year after year, century after century, age after age, if the conditions are not greatly altered, because the successor follows, in the course of its development, the same lines as its predecessor did. It is thus by hereditary transmission that the characters of plants are perpetuated.

Variation—Selection.—But the course of development in the offspring is not always and in all cases the same as in the parents. On the contrary, there is a certain range of variation, by virtue of which a seedling plant does not exactly reproduce either of the parental forms; indeed, as it is of mixed origin, it could not be expected to do so.

The limits of variation no one can tell; sometimes they seem very narrow; at other times we know them to be very wide. Within short periods of time the amount of variations may be inappreciable. Within geological periods the variation in the course of development is sometimes so enormous that, were there not evidence of the fact, it would be difficult to connect the plants and animals that have gone before with those which now exist. Living plants, then, are influenced in the course of their development by two somewhat antagonistic principles—the hereditary principle which, on the whole, tends to keep plants as they are, and the tendency to vary, which is the source of that variation in character which enables plants and animals gradually to become adapted to altered circumstances. This is beneficial to the cultivator, by affording him an opportunity of selecting the varieties best suited for his purpose. It is by exercising selection of this kind that Mr. Hallett succeeded in raising his "Pedigree Wheat." He simply selected for sowing the best grains from the largest and best ears, and repeated the process year after year, just as the gardener has done for countless generations in the case of fruits and seeds, as the cattle-breeder does with Shorthorns or other pedigree animals. These processes the farmer might with great advantage practice to a much greater extent than he usually does, and thus secure hardy productive varieties best suited to his particular conditions and best likely to fulfil his requirements.

Formation of the Embryo.—The two processes of growth and development may also be illustrated by recalling what takes place in the germination of a seed. A ripe seed contains within its coat or husk an embryo plant. Very often that embryo plant is invested, as in the case of the grain of wheat, with a whitish, floury substance, known as the "perisperm." All grass seeds have this perisperm surrounding their embryo. A similar substance is found in the seeds of mangel; the seeds of turnips, peas, beans, and clover, on the other hand, are destitute of it. An embryo plant consists of a radicle, or rudimentary root, surmounted by a caulicle, which is often so short as to be imperceptible to the naked eye, but from which spring the seed-leaves, or cotyledons—one only in the case of all the cereals and grasses, two in the case of the other crops of the farm. In the case of the wheat grain, where the perisperm is abundant, the cotyledon is small and thin; but in the pea or bean, where the perisperm is absent, the cotyledons are very thick and fleshy. The difference depends upon the presence, in the one case, of large quantities of reserve-materials in the embryo itself, while in the case of the wheat the reserve-materials are stored up in the perisperm.

The seed, then, in addition to the young plant, contains in the tissues of the embryo plant itself, or in the perisperm surrounding it, reserve-materials destined to supply the young plant with food during its growth and development.

Reserve-materials: their Transport. — Under the head of nutrition, mention has been made of the substances formed in plants through various agencies. Some of these are used up at once during growth, while others are reserved for future use, having usually undergone some change in constitution to fit them for their purpose. Speaking broadly, these reserves are either starchy, oily, or albuminoid (nitrogenous) in their character. The starchy or oily ingredients are the direct products of the action carried on under the influence of sun light in the cells containing chlorophyll. Starch cannot be formed in cells containing no chlorophyll, nor, for a continuance, in chlorophyll-containing cells, unless they are exposed to the light. The starch in a wheat grain, for instance, is not actually formed within the seed—it is formed in the leaves and conveyed from them to the seed. But starch is insoluble; therefore, before it can be conveyed from the place where it is formed to the place where it is to be stored, it must be rendered soluble, and this change is effected by a process of fermentation resulting in its conversion into soluble "glucose." Arrived at the seed, the glucose is turned back into insoluble starch to be reserved for use when required. The process is essentially the same in the case of the tuber of the potato, the "bulb" of the turnip, or the root of the mangel. All these organs are severally storehouses wherein food is accumulated for future use. The food is neither made nor elaborated in them, but simply stored, having been formed in the leaves and conveyed to the storehouse. At one time, therefore, the leaves and stem may be full of starch, at another, they may be destitute of it, owing to its having been transferred to the seed or the bulb.

While the origin of the starch is now well known and the processes connected with its formation and transport fairly understood, it is not so with the nitrogenous matters. The nitrogen, as we have seen, enters the plant by the root, and is, therefore, not directly dependent on light or chlorophyll action. Nitrogenous compounds are not formed in the seed, but conveyed to them just as the starch is.

The carbonaceous reserve-materials—that is, the starch, the sugar, the oil, the coloring matters—are all the direct result of the action of the green matter acted on by light; the starch and the sugar are essential requisites for the building up of the cell-membrane, the albuminoid or nitrogen-containing substances being, in their turn, essential to the formation of the protoplasm, and of the chlorophyll.

Germination.—The conditions under which germination takes place need not be alluded to at any length, as they are the same as those requisite for growth, and practically every cultivator knows that air (oxygen), moisture, and heat, varying in amount according to the plant and according to circumstances, are required, and that his success depends in great measure upon the proper tillage of the soil which secures these requisites. When the seed, or rather the embryo plant within it, begins to grow, water is absorbed, the seed swells, the insoluble starch stored up becomes converted into glucose, or a form of sugar, by the agency of a nitrogenous substance which acts as a ferment. These chemical processes are accompanied by an evolution of heat and an outpouring of carbonic acid gas. Thus is it that in malting barley the grain swells, gets hot, and its starch is converted into sugar. As the seedling grows, both starch and sugar gradually disappear, although the stock of starch is continually replenished so long as the leaves continue to act. The nitrogenous constituents of the seed undergo similar changes from the insoluble to the soluble condition, the latter being capable of transport from place to place as may be required.

The accumulation of insoluble matter in the seeds is accounted for by M. Dehérain in this wise. At the period of maturation the juices of the plant contain the various substances held in solution. These juices are directed towards the seed or towards the store organs, wherein, by virtue of some changes not fully understood, the matters previously held in solution become as it were precipitated and rendered for the time insoluble. As a consequence, the water is deprived of these materials, and to restore the balance fresh supplies are drafted from the leaves towards the store-organs, there in like manner to deposit their starch, their inulin, or albuminoid matter. In the case of biennials like turnips, or mangels, during the first season of growth, the leaves collect and form the nutritive matters which are subsequently transferred to the "root," and the store so accumulated is utilized the following season in the formation of flowers and seeds, as before explained.

Growth, then, in a chemical sense, may be said to consist in the absorption of the raw materials for the food of plants—development, in a chemical sense, may be taken as including the various transformations which those raw materials undergo to fit them for the nutrition of the plant, or the formation of reserve-materials to be stored up for future use. The history of these developmental changes is a matter for the chemist to clear up with the aid of chemical re-agents, used both with and without the help of the microscope. It is in this department of physiology that our knowledge is at present most imperfect.

Maturation.—The foregoing facts and phenomena have been brought to light principally by chemical analysis of the same kind of plant at different times and in different stages of its growth, and particularly by the analysis of different parts of the same plant, some young, some old. In the case of wheat, it was ascertained by Messrs. Lawes and Gilbert that during the five weeks beginning with June 21, there was but little accumulation of nitrogen in the plant, while during the same period more than half the total carbon was accumulated. The building-up process was thus going on more quickly than that of maturation. In this manner it has also been found, not only that the starchy and the albuminous matters undergo changes and disappear from the leaves, but that mineral matters and salts, such as phosphates and salts of potash, which at one stage of growth abound in the leaves, at another time are almost entirely absent from them, but are found in abundance elsewhere. The migration of these elements has been well studied in the case of the wheat by M. Isidore Pierre, who has conclusively shown that what the leaves lose in these respects is gained by the ear. One important feature of maturation then consists in the gradual cessation of the work done in the leaf, the exhaustion of its supplies—carbonaceous, nitrogenous, and mineral—and the transport of these materials to the organs of reserve, to the bark and young wood of the tree, to the seed in the case of wheat and other annuals, to the roots, bulbs, and tubers in other cases. In the case of an annual herbaceous plant like the wheat it appears that both root-action and leaf-action become reduced to a minimum, or are even altogether stopped some two or three weeks before the wheat is ready to cut, so that during that period no increase of weight of the plant as a whole takes place; and if the ears themselves increase in weight, it is because they derive matter from other parts of the plant, which diminish in weight in proportion. A few figures cited by M. Dehérain will illustrate the truth of these remarks—thus in the case of colza, out of a total of one thousand parts (grammes) of phosphoric acid in the entire plant, four hundred and fifty-six were found in the leaves in March, and only twenty-five in the leaves in June, while the flowering stems at the latter period contained eight hundred and sixty. Results of a similar character might be quoted in the case of potash and albuminoid matters. In all cases while the relative proportions gradually decline in the leaves they become correspondingly augmented in the flowering part of the stem and in the seeds.

These results are attributed by M. Dehérain in great degree to varying degrees of evaporating power possessed by the leaves. According to him, the older leaves at the base of the stem evaporate but little as compared to the younger leaves near the top. These, by their superior evaporating power, cause the lower parts to be emptied of their contents, which are thus forced upwards towards the upper part of the stem. In a very dry, hot season, when the light is intense, evaporation and life-action generally go on too rapidly, and the harvest is deficient; on the other hand, if the summer is wet and the light deficient, maturation is imperfect, the transport of nutritive matters from leaves upwards to the fruit and seeds is checked, the younger leaves do not draw upon the lower ones, and the season, though favorable to forage crops, is not so propitious to grain crops, to fruit ripening, or to timber in which a deposit of woody material in the cells is essential.

Ripening of Fruits.—The ripening of fruits, such as those of the apple and pear is attended with a series of chemical changes which can here only be cursorily alluded to. While the fruit remains green, it acts precisely as a leaf does. As it ripens its color changes; it no longer decomposes carbonic acid and gives off oxygen in the daylight, but it utilizes the oxygen of the carbonic acid to oxidize and burn up the vegetable acid and the sugar which the fruit contains. Subsequently the sugar undergoes a species of alcoholic fermentation, characterized by the emission of carbonic acid gas and by the formation of alcohol, which latter, uniting with the acid of the fruit, produces ethers of various kinds, to which the peculiar odor and flavor of the fruit are due.

The processes of maturation and fruiting therefore are not dependent upon the mere accumulation of food; otherwise by increasing the quantity of manure and applying it continuously we should increase the crop. As a matter of fact we know we should not do so, and that the effect of over-feeding under such circumstances would be to render the plant unhealthy by preventing it from assimilating and maturing. Similarly we know from experience that heat alone is not sufficient to induce thorough ripening, but that exposure to light is also requisite, a dull, cloudy summer, even if warm, being unpropitious to ripening, whether of fruit or grain.

CHAPTER VI.

MULTIPLICATION.

Sub-division.—Intermarriage.—Buds, Branches, Tillering, Tubers.—Fertilization, Stamens, Anthers, Pollen, Pistil.—Mechanism of Fertilization. — Cross-Fertilization. — Transport of Pollen. — Insect agency.—Self-Fertilization.—Fertilization of cereals.—Hybridization.—Germination.

Multiplication.—There are two special ways in which plants multiply. One is a mere process of extension or subdivision—a modified form of growth, in fact. The other is the result of the union or commingling of a portion of the protoplasm of one plant with a corresponding particle of another plant. In the lower plants, as they are designated, it is not even necessary that union of particles of protoplasm from different plants should be effected. The contents of one cell blend with the contents of another cell on the same plant, and the result is the formation of a seed or spore, by means of which the plant is reproduced. The first process of multiplication, by division, is called asexual, the second sexual, because it is a process of intermarriage requiring the co-operation of two distinct particles of protoplasm. In the very lowest plants these two particles present no appreciable differences, but in the higher plants and animals they present such differences as to enable us to distinguish one as male, the other as female. In the lowest plant the two particles are split off from the same mass of protoplasm, while in the higher plants the male element is formed from a different source from the female.

Bud Formation. — In the higher perennial plants, among which are included many which come under the notice of the farmer, asexual multiplication is effected by means of buds. When a bud is to be formed, growth in length is checked, the stem or the branch ceases lengthening, the outer leaves often become reduced to a scale-like condition, while the inner, central, and younger ones remain in an undeveloped state until the warmth of spring calls them into growth, when they gradually lengthen into shoots, as in fruit and timber trees. While the buds remain fixed to the trees which gave them origin, their growth and development is a process of extention or branching merely. Similarly the process of "tillering" is simply due to the formation and development of buds and shoots from the nodes or knots at the base of the stem of the wheat, and is to be regarded as a process of branching rather than of actual multiplication. Such branches are formed more readily in proportion as the seed is not buried deeply. The same process of growth which is desirable in a cereal or in clover is highly objectionable in the case of "weeds," such as docks, thistles, and plantains. The imperfect measures often taken to exterminate these often tend to increase the mischief by bringing about the formation of many new buds. When buds become detached naturally, or are severed from the parent artificially and made to grow — as when a gardener takes a "slip," "buds" a rose, or "grafts" a fruit tree — the process is really one of multiplication. So, when a farmer plants a "seed potato," which yields him, it may be, forty-fold, he really plants, not a "seed," nor a root, but a peculiar form of bud called a tuber.

Tubers. — A potato, in fact, is an underground branch, or connected series of buds, forming a swollen subterranean shoot. In this are stored up the starch and other ingredients necessary for the nutrition of the young potato plants. The "eyes" of the potato are really buds, as any one may see for himself who will examine the "chits" of a sprouting potato. These latter bear the same relation to the parent tuber that the shoots which spring from the old "stools" in a coppice or from a pollard willow do to the trunk. The presence of these tubers indicates that, under natural circumstances, the plant requires a long period of rest. To this end food is stored in the tuber, and active growth ceases for a time, until again excited by heat and moisture. It may be inferred from this that continuous growth, were it possible, would be injurious because the climatal conditions are unsuited for it, as, indeed, may be witnessed in the way in which the haulms of the early potatoes are injured by spring frost.

Fertilization.—In the case of plants grown for their fruit or seed, as in the case of wheat and cereals generally, much attention has naturally to be paid to the conditions which favor sexual multiplication.

The morphological characters of the plants undergo a change. In general terms, it may be said that the growth of the stem is arrested, and the growth and mode of development of the leaves not only arrested, but more or less profoundly modified, so as to form the parts of the flower. All parts of the flower are constructed on the same original plan as leaves, but they gradually assume a very different appearance in the course of their development to fit them for their work of aiding fertilization. It is not necessary in this place to enter into details as to the floral construction, which varies in different plants; the important points in relation to our present subject are the stamens and the pistils and their contents.

Within the green scales which constitute the flower of

wheat, within the butterfly-shaped and brightly-colored petals of the pea or the clovers, and the yellow petals of the flowers of the turnip or the colza, the rape or the mustard, are a series of fine thread-like bodies, the "stamens," varying in number, size, and arrangement in different flowers, but each consisting of a fine thread or stalk, called the "filament." Surmounting this is a sort of pocket or case, called the "anther," containing a yellow or greenish dust, which, when examined with a lens, is seen to be made up of separate cells or grains, called the pollen grains. Some idea of the number of these pollen grains may be gained from the calculations of Mr. A. S. Wilson, who estimates, from the actual counting of a portion, that each anther of rye contains twenty thousand pollen cells, five hundred thousand of which are needed to make up one grain in weight. A floret of spring wheat in like manner was found to contain six thousand eight hundred and sixty-four grains, but, as the pollen grains of the wheat are larger than those of the rye, only three hundred and ninety thousand are required to make up a grain weight. An acre of wheat may, it is further calculated, produce fifty pounds of pollen, and an acre of rye two hundred and twenty-four pounds.

Within the stamens, in most flowers with which farmers have to do, is a "pistil," consisting of a thick portion below, which contains the young "ovule" destined to become the seed, and which is usually overtopped by a little thread, called the "style," whose upper end, again, is dilated into a "stigma." In the case of the wheat and other grasses these stigmas are covered with fine white, silky hairs. The essential constituents of the flower, without which reproduction cannot be effected, are the pollen grains and the ovule. All other parts of the flower are mere accessories, and some of them are very frequently absent without the process of reproduction being impaired by their absence.

The process of fertilization may be described in general terms as follows:—The ovule contains, in a cell just beneath the skin at its summit, one special piece of protoplasm, the "germ," which is destined to develop into the embryo plant. The pollen-cell consists of an outer coat and an inner lining; the outer coat bursts, and the inner protoplasmic lining is protruded in the form of a tube, which passes down between the cells of the stigma and style, growing in length and feeding as it goes, like a parasitic fungus, on the contents of the cells of the style, until it reaches the ovule and comes into close proximity to, if not actually into contact with the germ. In consequence of this action a cell-wall is formed around the germ, which latter divides and subdivides in various directions, the result of the subdivision being the formation of an embryo plant, as mentioned at p. 74, while the ovule covering the embryo ripens into the seed. The germ is thus fertilized by the pollen or sperm-cell, and unless the two come in contact, the formation of the embryo plant does not take place.

Cross Fertilization.—It has been mentioned that the flowers with which the farmer is concerned have for the most part their stamens and pistils in the same flower (hops are an exception*), and therefore they may be described as structurally hermaphrodite. It does not, however, follow that they are functionally hermaphrodite—that is, that the pollen-grain of any particular flower fertilizes the germ-cell of the same flower. As a matter of fact, the reverse usually happens, and the pollen of

---

*In the hop, the stamens and pistils are in separate flowers upon different plants. The farmer in the United States will find that the stamens and pistils are in different flowers upon the same plant in Indian corn, pumpkin, squash, and all other plants of that family.

one flower exerts its influence, not upon the germ of its own flower, but upon that of another, perhaps situated on some other plant. Cross-fertilization is often necessitated by the circumstance that while the pollen of any particular flower may be ripe, the stigma and the germ-cell of the same flower may not be ripe at the same time, or *vice versa,* and in such case the co-operation of some other flower is needed.

Transport of Pollen.—It becomes, therefore, needful to ascertain in what manner the pollen is carried from one flower to another. This is effected in various ways—sometimes the mere splitting of the anther with some degree of force suffices to scatter the pollen, at other times the currents of air suffice to waft it from one flower to another, while at other times insects of various kinds convey the pollen from one flower and deposit it on the stigma of another.

The adaptations of floral structure to insect-agency in fertilization, as also the contrivances for excluding undesirable visitors, are most varied and most remarkable, but they can only be mentioned here. As a rule, it may be stated that flowers endowed with bright colors, irregular construction (like that of the pea or bean), or rich perfume are fertilized by insect agency. The insects are attracted by the bright colors, the perfumes, and the sweet secretions of the flower. On alighting, they are often compelled by the peculiar construction and mechanism of the flower to enter or leave it in such a way that they must in the one case brush out the pollen, and in the other deposit it on the stigma. It will be noted how this process of cross-fertilization favors that process of variation to which allusion has previously been made.

The farmer wishing to keep his stock of seed turnips pure, knows how difficult it is to do this, not only because cross-fertilization is the rule in the particular variety he wishes to grow, but also because, if any other variety is grown in the neighborhood, its pollen is sure to impregnate his variety and produce a mongrel offspring. Cross-fertilization then acts in antagonism to the hereditary tendency, and secures variation—and not only variation, but more vigorous and robust constitution, and more numerous and more healthy descendants.

Self-fertilization, or "in and in breeding," occurs, no doubt, in some instances, especially in cereal grasses; and there are indeed many cases where, for various reasons which need not be cited here, no other mode of fertilization is possible. Relative permanence of character is secured by this means, and if constitutional vigor and the health of the offspring be impaired by the long continuance of the process, these ill-effects are provided against by the circumstance that a comparatively trifling change in the flower, or in the circumstances by which it is surrounded, will suffice to prevent self-fertilization and secure cross-fertilization.

Fertilization of Cereals.—It has very generally been stated that the wind is the special agency by means of which the pollen is carried from flower to flower of these plants, and no doubt this is true to some extent and under certain circumstances. From the careful experiments and observations of Mr. A. S. Wilson, recorded in a paper read before the Botanical Society of Edinburgh, Scotland, and printed in the "Gardener's Chronicle," March 14, 1874, it appears that self-fertilization is the rule among cereals, though cross-fertilization does occasionally take place and has been effected artificially by various experimenters. The flowers of wheat, barley, and oats open to a slight degree and allow the anthers to protrude, often quite suddenly; but whether the flowers fully or but partially open, says Mr. W., they are fertilized before the anthers are visible outside. "The Belgian farmers," he continues, "who trailed ropes over their flowering wheat to insure complete fertilization, were doing that which the very appearance of the anthers told them in whispers, not yet heard, had already been accomplished." The pollen of these plants which the winds disperse, is not that which fertilizes, but that which is not required for fertilization. The success of the process depends, as before said, upon the circumstance whether or not the pollen and the feathery stigma are respectively ripe at the same time. If so, then fertilization results; if not, there is still a chance of cross-fertilization, but if that fail, the flower remains barren.

Hybridization is a procedure with which the gardener is much more familiar than the farmer. It is only a further development of cross-fertilization. Cross-fertilization, as has been said, takes place between flowers of the same individual plant, or between flowers of two different individuals of the same species; but hybridization is effected by crossing the flowers of two separate species, as in the case of the Alsike clover, which is said to be a hybrid between the white or Dutch clover and the red clover.

Chemical Changes.—The chemical changes which occur during the formation of the flower, and especially during the ripening of the seed, have already been alluded to. The contrast between the composition of the leaves and that of the pollen and of the seeds is very striking, and analysis brings out the fact of the accumulation of nitrogenous and phosphatic and mineral matters in the pollen and in the seed. In haymaking it is better, if possible, to mow before the leaves are exhausted of their contents by the seeds, or at any rate, before the latter are shed. If cutting be delayed, a great part of the nutritive matter is withdrawn from the leaves and stem to be stored up in the seeds, which fall readily when ripe, and thus occasion a loss to the farmer. Again, as it has been shown that the seeds of cereals contain their full proportion of nutritive matter some little time before they would be considered thoroughly ripe, early cutting, where practicable, is to be recommended to secure the crop and obviate possible loss from delay.

CHAPTER VII.

THE BATTLE OF LIFE.

Plants considered in their relation to their struggle for existence.—Effect of adverse external conditions.—Hostility of rivals, Weeds.—Competition of fellows.—Gregarious vegetation. —Associated or mixed vegetation.—Alternate vegetation, rotation.—Objects of the cultivator not the same as those of the plant under natural circumstances.—The battle as studied in pasture-land or meadow.—The grass-plots at Rothamsted—their botanical composition and the way they are affected by manures of different kinds.—The Grasses, their nature and differences; contrasts between nearly allied species.—The Leguminosæ.—The Miscellaneous weeds.—The vegetation and characteristics of the continuously unmanured plot.—The effects of different manures and of different combinations of manures upon the struggle.—Effects of disuse of manure, and of the substitution of one kind for another.—General results.

In former sections mention has been made of the relations which the living plant bears to the heat, light, moisture, and other physical conditions, by which it is surrounded. These conditions are sometimes favorable, sometimes prejudicial. In the latter case, the existence of the plant becomes a prolonged struggle against adverse influences. To a certain extent it is always so, and when the difficulties can no longer be counterbalanced or overcome, plants, like other living beings, succumb and die. The life of each individual then may be described as a battle against circumstances.

But apart from this external conflict with the elements, plants are always more or less in a state of internecine war. Plants of different kinds growing wild in a state of nature may contend one with another for root-hold, soil-food, and for space to expose their foliage to the sun. Under such circumstances, if there is enough for all, it may be that the severity of the struggle may be slight, owing to the different requirements of the different plants, but even then the stronger of the two will eventually prevail. A farmer, however, would hardly call the preponderance of weeds an instance of the survival of the fittest. From his point of view it would certainly not be so, however true it might be in wild nature. Plants of the same kind growing gregariously, like heaths on a moor, have the same requirements, and these are supplied in about equal proportions to all the individual plants. The result is that while the weak ones are crowded out, the survivors are all pretty much on an equality; but once the balance is destroyed, then that which is the stronger, or the one best adapted to the circumstances under which it is placed, will survive.

In cultivation we have illustrations of mixed and of gregarious vegetation in the sense above employed, as well as of alternate vegetation as in the case of "rotation." In the case of the cereals, of turnips, of potatoes, and others, we have instances of gregarious vegetation induced, indeed, by the will of the cultivator. His object is to secure the most profitable development of one particular kind of plant, wheat, barley, oats, or what not. To compass this end he grows them together, takes means by appropriate tillage, and by the removal of competing weeds, to enhance the conditions most favorable to their growth and to minimize the effects of those that are injurious. The warfare here is external as regards "weeds," it is internecine between individual plants of the same species and having the same requirements. As the competition of alien plants may be prevented by weeding, so internecine war between plant and plant of the same kind may be mitigated by the adoption of thin seeding, which allows each individual to attain its complete development, and enables it to avail itself to the full of the resources at its disposal. Unless under exceptional circumstances and for some special purpose, it is more profitable so to grow plants as to diminish the competition between individuals by affording each the best possible chance. Otherwise, the strongest or best adapted prevails, indeed, over those less favorably situate, but there is, so far as the cultivator is concerned, a loss of energy and a waste of resource in the case of the beaten plants. The cultivator requires for his purpose the largest number of plants of good average quality; nature favors the development of a few of exceptional power of adaptation, which therefore overcome their fellows, but which are not necessarily the best for the farmer.

The Battle in the Meadow.—The battle of life is perhaps best studied in mixed pastures where a great variety of plants of different families, different construction, and different requirements are grown in association. In such pastures some of the constituent plants are valuable to the farmer, as some of the grasses and most of the leguminous plants; others are relatively useless and may be positively injurious. The behavior of the different classes of plants so growing in association, but under varied conditions of manuring, for a large number of years, has been made the subject of prolonged and elaborate study at Rothamsted. A few of the leading results may here be mentioned in merest outline for the purpose of illustrating the subject of this chapter, and of affording matters for consideration by the practical cultivator.

The total number of different kinds of plants that have been found on the plots is eighty-nine, of which twenty are grasses, ten leguminous, and the remainder, occurring usually in smaller proportions and belonging to many natural orders, are conveniently grouped as "miscellaneous." The numbers and relative proportions of these, as noted in the growing herbage or recognized in the samples taken from it, differ very much in different seasons, and more especially according to the nature of the manure employed.

The plants vary among themselves, the grasses having certain characters in common, the leguminous plants differing from the grasses, and both more or less from the miscellaneous plants, the members of which latter group differ very considerably among themselves. The variations alluded to depends of course on the varying organization, hereditary endowments, internal structure, habit, constitution, and mode of life of the several plants. Some of these points are much more influenced by external conditions of soil and climate than others.

The Grasses.*–Of the eighteen grasses which commonly occur on the plots all are perennial except *Bromus mollis*.

---

* In the text the Latin names of the plants mentioned are employed as more precise and uniform in their application, not varying in different localities, and being in universal use in botanical works; but as these names may not be familiar to some readers, the most commonly adopted English names are here supplied. It should be remembered that only the more important of the pasture plants are here alluded to.

[The common names most in use in the United States are added in brackets.]

Grasses.

Anthoxanthum odoratum	— Sweet vernal grass.
Alopecurus pratensis	— Meadow fox tail grass.
Phleum pratense	— Meadow cat's-tail. [Timothy.]
Agrostis vulgaris	— Florin grass. [Red-top.]
Aira cæspitosa	— Tussack or hair grass.
Holcus lanatus	— Woolly soft grass.
Avena pubescens	— Downy oat-grass.
" elatior	— False oat-grass.

They occur in very varying proportions on the different plots according to the season and according to the nature of the manure employed. They vary somewhat in robustness of constitution and ability to withstand frost or drouth; and their structural characters are, generally speaking, characteristically different from those of other plants, and variable as between species and species. Some maintain their ground or even increase when growing in competition or association with their fellows; others—such as *Anthoxanthum odoratum, Festuca ovina,* and *Agrostis vulgaris*—can only hold their own or assert themselves when the competition exercised by their associates is relatively weak, and succumb under the opposite circumstances.

Avena flavescens	—	Yellow oat-grass.
Poa pratensis	—	Meadow grass. [Blue grass.]
" trivialis	—	Rough stalked meadow grass.
Briza media	—	Quake-grass.
Dactylis glomerata	—	Cock's-foot grass. [Orchard G.]
Cynosurus cristatus	—	Crested dog's-tail grass.
Festuca ovina	—	Sheeps' fescue.
" pratensis	—	Meadow fescue.
" elatior	—	Tall fescue.
Bromus mollis	—	Soft brome grass.
Lolium perenne	—	Rye grass.

LEGUMINOSÆ.

Trifolium repens	—	White clover.
" pratense	—	Meadow clover. [Red clover.]
Lotus corniculatus	—	Bird's-foot trefoil.
Lathyrus pratensis	—	Meadow vetchling.

WEEDS.

Ranunculus–various species—		Buttercups.
Cerastium triviale	—	Mouse-ear chickweed.
Conopodium denudatum	—	Earth nut.
Centaurea nigra	—	Knap-weed.
Carduus arvensis	—	Common thistle. [Canada T.]
Bellis perennis	—	Daisy.
Achillea Millefolium	—	Milfoil. [Yarrow.]
Taraxacum officinale	—	Dandelion.
Plantago lanceolata	—	Plantain or Rib grass.
Rumex Acetosa	—	Sorrel-dock.

The grasses, both in number of species and in relative and actual amount of produce, exceed the plants of all other orders. The lowest produce occurs on the continuously unmanured plots; the highest on those to which a highly nitrogenous manure, such as ammonia salts or nitrate of soda, is continuously applied in combination with earthy and alkaline salts—especially potash. But while the total gramineous produce is thus increased by the description of manure just mentioned, the number of species of grass is reduced. On the unmanured plots, on the average, sixteen different sorts of grasses may be found, each contributing a fair proportion to the total herbage; thirteen only are found on the highly ammoniated plots, and of these only a very few contribute materially to the crop, the remainder being present in such small quantities as to make but little difference in the totals.

The principal external characteristics which favor the growth of the grasses in their competition with other plants are their dense root-growth, monopolizing as it were all the soil within reach, and affording little power to the roots of other plants to penetrate the mass. To an extent variable in different species, this root-growth is both superficial as well as deep. In addition to this generally ample root development, many of the species are aided in the struggle by their stout tufted habit and specially by their power of producing creeping offshoots above or below ground which insinuate themselves in between other plants and occupy any vacant territory. No doubt internal anatomical differences are even of greater moment than these external characteristics, but these demand minute comparative study by means of the microscope, under various conditions, and at different seasons, and constitute a branch of inquiry at present hardly even entered upon.

Although grasses as a whole comport themselves in a

particular manner distinct from that of the other tenants of the plot, yet it is found that individual grasses, and even members of the same genus, vary very much among one another.

It is instructive to compare the different tendencies of the two most generally prevalent grasses, *Festuca ovina* and *Agrostis vulgaris*. As to structural endowments they would seem to be not unfairly matched, but the *Festuca* is conspicuously worsted on the plots highly dressed with nitrogenous manures, while the *Agrostis* is befriended by them, and its vigor and tufted habit are increased. *Poa trivialis* and *Holcus lanatus* afford contrasts of a similar character, the *Poa* being largely increased by nitrate of soda, while the *Holcus* is similarly acted on by ammonia salts. Of the same character are the differences observable between *Agrostis vulgaris*, which is influenced by ammonia salts, and *Holcus lanatus*, *Avena pubescens*, and *Avena flavescens*, which are especially acted upon by nitrate of soda. Very marked contrasts between species of the same genus also occur, as between such structurally very closely related plants as *Poa trivialis*, and *P. pratensis*, and between the three species of *Avena*. On the contrary, *Bromus mollis* and *Poa trivialis* are so far similar that nitrate of soda is very favorable to them both. *Poa pratensis* and *Agrostis vulgaris* concur in their liking for ammonia with mineral salts, while they manifest opposite tendencies with regard to nitrate of soda; *Poa pratensis* not being favored by it, while the *Agrostis* is so conspicuously.

These are only a few of the remarkable contrasts and similarities that an inspection of the Rothamsted records brings out. Perhaps the most striking point in this connection is the opposite tendency manifested by different grasses in reference to the action of ammonia salts, and of nitrate of soda respectively, with or without mineral manures in addition in each case. Doubtless, these characteristics are to be correlated with differences of organization and structure, but with the exception that the shallower rooted plants are often favored by ammonia salts, and the deeper rooting ones by the more deeply percolating nitrate, little or nothing has been done in definitely associating the different physiological endowments above referred to, with corresponding differences of internal structure.

The **Leguminosæ** form a group of plants characterized, so far as this country is concerned, by the presence of "papilionaceous" flowers like those of the common pea, by their leaves being compound, *i. e.*, consisting of separable segments, and by the production of a seed-pod, which, when ripe, splits into two valves or flaps; this is technically called a "legume." By these characteristics, not to mention others, this group which comprises peas, beans, clovers, vetches, sainfoin, lucerne, and other agricultural plants, may be known. Some, such as peas and beans are annual, others are perennial, and, as a rule, their habit or general appearance is so strikingly different from that of the grasses, that no one ever confounds them.

Though containing a larger proportion of nitrogen in their composition than the cereals, they are not specially benefited by nitrogenous manures as the grasses are, and this fact, observed when Leguminosæ are grown alone, as in the bean or clover field, is no less marked than it is when they are grown in association as in pasture land. At Rothamsted, the largest proportionate quantities of Leguminosæ occur on a plot to which mixed mineral manure with potash is applied. Seasonal characteristics, even when favorable to these plants, do not suffice to overcome the injurious effects of some manures, as during many years of varying character as to climate, they have been practically banished from the ammonia plots. On the whole their requirements are opposite to those of the grasses, the conditions favoring the latter not being anything like so propitious to the leguminous plants. Thus the effect of nitrogenous manures as observed on the experimental plots is to banish or reduce more or less completely the Leguminosæ, or so to favor the growth of the grasses, or certain of them, that the Leguminosæ are overpowered. On the other hand, mineral manures, which are not by themselves very beneficial to grasses, are very propitious to the growth of leguminous plants. Potash is especially favorable to these plants, their predominance and produce is always enhanced when that substance is used in due proportions as a manure, and always diminished when it is omitted. In illustration, it may be added, that on the plot where the manurial conditions are most favorable to Leguminosæ, the weight per cent of the whole crop was as follows :—Sixty-five per cent grasses, twenty per cent leguminous, and fifteen per cent miscellaneous. The per-centage by weight on the unmanured plot was, sixty-eight grasses, nine leguminous, and twenty-three miscellaneous. Taking the other extreme where a large quantity of nitrogenous manure was employed, the figures are ninety-five per cent grasses, and five per cent miscellaneous, the Leguminosæ being all but absent (one per cent).

Of the Leguminosæ of pasture-land *Lathyrus pratensis* seems to be able to hold its own under adverse conditions much better than its fellows, the clovers or the Lotus. Its long, straggling root, and scrambling habit added to its hardihood may be the source of these advantages.

Miscellaneous Plants.—In spite of the large number and varied habits of growth of the miscellaneous species found on the plots, their importance as factors in tho struggle is less than that of the grasses and of the leguminous plants. The proportion in which they occur on the several manured plots is always less than that of the grasses, and they never really attain any very great degree of prominence, except in cases where from seasonal or manurial causes the grasses are prevented from attaining their full development. Those species which, like *Rumex Acetosa*, have a powerful underground development, and abundant capacity for collecting and storing water, etc., of course have an advantage especially when it so happens that they can avail themselves of unoccupied territory, which they seize and hold with great success against all comers, and also in cases where the density of the soil is such as to offer an obstacle to the penetration of fibrous roots. But, on the whole, the dense fibrous net-work of roots made by the grasses, which enables them to avail themselves of well nigh every particle of soil within their reach, is a more valuable possession than is the more robust underground rootstock possessed by several of the miscellaneous plants. Most of the species occur in too insignificant amounts to be considered as anything more than accidental tenants, and while in others their preponderance depends on the relative inferiority of the growth of grasses, there are also indications that some of them are favorably affected by certain manures, and others by fertilizing agents of different character. But on the whole, these indications observed on plants growing in association are by no means so marked as in the cases of the grasses and the Leguminosæ.

Growth of Pasture Plants when unaffected by manure of any kind.—The changes from year to year in the vegetation of a plot which has been unmanured for many years must obviously be mainly due to seasonal influences, and progressive exhaustion of the soil, while those which are observed in the manured plots are as obviously brought about, partly by the manures and partly by climatal changes. The produce of hay at Rothamsted, without manure, has varied from eight hundred and ninety-six pounds, to four thousand three hundred and sixty-eight pounds, the average for twenty-five years having been, as before stated, two thousand five hundred and seventy-six pounds per acre. This hay is made up on the average of forty-nine different species in different proportions, as determined by rigid comparative scrutiny. Of the forty-nine plants, seventeen are grasses, four leguminous plants, and the remaining twenty-eight are pasture weeds of various orders, and roughly classified as miscellaneous plants. By weight, grasses furnished sixty-nine per cent, Leguminosæ eight, and miscellaneous plants twenty-three per cent of the total produce.

The general appearance of the unmanured plots is one of even growth, with no special luxuriance of any particular plant. The herbage is very mixed, the crop scanty, the color yellowish-green, in fact a sort of trades-union equality is produced, between the different members of the community, no one kind being specially favored. *Festuca ovina* usually predominates among the grasses. *Briza media* is more abundant on these plots than on most others. Among the leguminous plants, *Lotus corniculatus* is more prevalent than *Lathyrus pratensis*, as is usually found to be the case when there is soil exhaustion and a deficiency of potash. The miscellaneous plants are generally very abundant, such as the buttercups. *Plantago lanceolata, Centaurea nigra, Agrimonia Eupatoria, Scabiosa arvensis, Leontodon hispidus, Prunella vulgaris, Achillea Millefolium, Conopodium denudatum, Rumex Acetosa, Luzula campestris,* and *Galium verum.* The contrast in early summer between the scanty yellowish-green herbage, profusion of flowers of the various weeds, and the almost total absence of flowers and rich, deep blue-green foliage of the plants in the adjacent ammonia plot is very striking.

The effects of manure upon the struggle.—When in a long series of years the effects on the vegetation of a particular plot are observed to be uniform in their nature, if not in degree, the effects are obviously attributable to the manure employed, and the fluctuations are as clearly dependent on climatal variations. In endeavoring to give an idea of the effect of different manures in influencing the nature and fierceness of the struggle, it will be convenient to allude first to those cases in which no change has been made in the condition of manuring, mentioning first those plots in which comparatively simple manures are employed, and afterwards those in which a more complex manure is employed.

Mineral manures alone.—One of the plots at Rothamsted illustrates the effects of mineral manures consisting of admixtures of various earthy and alkaline salts used by themselves, without the admixture of nitrogenous substances. Speaking generally, it is there observed that, while graminaceous herbage has, with much fluctuation, slightly increased, the proportionate amount of leguminous plants, as compared with grasses, has on the whole been largely increased, although latterly it has shown a tendency to decline. The large increase is mainly due to *Lathyrus pratensis*, which prevails over all its fellows. The grasses which hold their own best are *Festuca ovina, Agrostis vulgaris,* and *Holcus lanatus.* *Achillea Millefolium* has increased considerably, *Conopodium denudatum* and *Rumex Acetosa*, have usually been abundant. This description of manure seems unfavorable to most of the weeds of pasture-land other than the above mentioned. The crop is generally moderate, with an even and early ripening, and a marked tendency to stemmy as distinguished from leafy growth, the color of the foliage being of a light, yellowish-green.

On the wheat plots, it has been shown that purely mineral manures scarcely increase the yield at all, though they are beneficial to the leguminous crops. These experiments confirm Boussingault's assertion that alkaline or earthy salts, although indispensable to plants, nevertheless, exercise no action unless combined with matters capable of furnishing nitrogen.

Superphosphate of lime only.—The scanty and stemmy produce on the plot, to which this substance is applied, has been but little greater than that on the unmanured plots. The grasses and miscellaneous plants have been slightly increased, the Leguminosæ diminished. There has been a great admixture of species, but little luxuriance of any. *Holcus lanatus, Avena flavescens, Poa trivialis, Lolium perenne*, and *Festuca ovina* have been among the most prominent grasses, while the freer-growing *Dactylis* does not apparently find so much subsistence as it requires. *Lathyrus pratensis* among the leguminous plants, and *Rumex Acetosa* and *Achillea Millefolium* among the weeds, have but slightly benefited, others yielding even less than without manure. Boussingault's observations, already quoted under the head of mineral manures, apply equally here. The great French chemist found, as in the Rothamsted experiments, that superphosphate, uncombined with substances capable of yielding ammonia, produced little or no effect on vegetation. Bœhm's experiments, however, go to show that young plants raised in distilled water, die before the nutritious matter stored up in the seed, or in the seed-leaves is exhausted, but if lime be added, especially in the form of ulmate, before this point is reached, the seedlings resume their healthy appearance, the development of the radicle, according to Dehérain, being particularly favored by this substance. (See p. 18).

Superphosphate has been proved to be of little or no use to other crops grown separately, except in the case of turnips, where about eight tons per acre have been produced by the use of superphosphate; the produce without manure at all, being one to two tons per acre.

Ammonia Alone.—The average produce with ammonia salts alone has not been very much greater than that on the unmanured plots. The principal differences are in the grasses, which have diminished as to number of species, but largely increased in proportionate amount to the other plants. *Agrostis vulgaris*, and especially *Festuca ovina*, both poor grasses, are so greatly favored, that they constitute the bulk of the crop, while other better grasses have diminished, even *Dactylis glomerata* not being by any means prominent. Ammonia salts are not propitious to any of the Leguminosæ, but *Lotus corniculatus* has had slightly the advantage over the others. Among the miscellaneous plants which, like the Leguminosæ, are well-nigh banished, *Rumex Acetosa* had the advantage; *Conopodium denudatum* also seems to have benefited in some seasons. The crop is generally moderate, of a rich, green color, and late in ripening, with much foliage, and relatively little tendency to flower.

Nitrate of Soda alone.—The general results of the application of this salt have been an increased proportion of grasses, particularly of *Festuca ovina*, *Alopecurus pratensis*, *Holcus lanatus* and *Poa trivialis*, *P. pratensis* being scarcely represented. There is in general not much tendency to form stem among the grasses. Leguminosæ exist in but scanty proportions, but among them *Lotus corniculatus* seems to have slightly the advantage. In the case of beans grown separately, nitrate of soda, unlike ammonia, is found to be beneficial. Among miscellaneous plants, *Rumex Acetosa* and *Centaurea nigra*, are specially noteworthy for their abundance; Ranunculi are also in fair quantity. *Plantago* has diminished, but the most remarkable feature is the enormous quantity of *Cerastium triviale* produced under the influence of this manure.

Nitrate of soda gives a late-ripening dark green crop, more leafy than stemmy in character, but nevertheless showing a greater disposition to form stem than in the case of plants treated with ammonia.

Superphosphate and Ammonia.—The effects produced by this combination, have corresponded to those which are met with in other plots to which ammonia is added, viz., increased produce, chiefly of graminaceous herbage, greatly diminished leguminous herbage, and relative absence of miscellaneous plants. *Festuca ovina* has enormously increased, and, to a less extent, the hardy creeping *Agrostis vulgaris*. On the other hand *Anthoxanthum odoratum, Holcus lanatus,* and *Avena pubescens,* have decreased. The crop is usually later in ripening than in the case of that to which the superphosphate alone is applied, and with more dark green leaf and less stem, characters which indicate the presence of ammonia.

Minerals and Ammonia.—In all the plots to which ammonia and minerals have been continuously applied, the produce is large, the per-centage and weight of grasses large, those of leguminous plants small or *nil*, and those of miscellaneous weeds also small. These effects are greater and more observable, the larger the quantity of ammonia, though the effects are by no means doubled in intensity, when the quantity of ammonia is doubled. The average produce has been larger than that of the other plots. The number of species has diminished, especially in the case of miscellaneous plants. Where the ammonia was in relatively slight proportions, *Festuca* *ovina, Agrostis vulgaris, Avena elatior, Holcus lanatus* and *Poa pratensis*, are noted to have been predominant, *Poa trivialis*, on the contrary, being practically banished. The two first-named plants owe their predominance not exclusively to the manure, for they thrive luxuriantly under many other conditions. A similar remark applies to *Rumex Acetosa*. On those plots where the quantity of ammonia salts was doubled, *Dactylis glomerata* for some years was in enormous preponderance, *Agrostis vulgaris, Holcus lanatus, Alopecurus pratensis* and *Avena elatior* have been also in large quantities. *Briza media. Cynosurus cristatus, Lolium perenne, Bromus mollis*, all poor grasses, except Lolium, have been discouraged by the ammonia. *Poa trivialis* also has greatly diminished in proportion to the quantity of *P. pratensis*.

Among the miscellaneous plants, Ranunculaceæ, like the Leguminosæ, have been practically banished. Umbelliferæ have been almost expelled, Compositæ largely diminished, Labiates greatly reduced; *Plantago lanceolata* is unrepresented, and even *Rumex Acetosa* considerably diminished. As these or corresponding effects are generally observed where ammonia forms part of the manure employed, and as they are enhanced when the quantity is increased (though not in direct proportion), it would seem that ammonia must be actually prejudicial to some plants. It is probable, however, that the diminished proportion of these plants is more often due to the increased luxuriance of the stronger-growing grasses than to the directly prejudicial effects of the manures on the other plants.

It is generally observed, that on the ammonia plots the plants show a great tendency to form leaves, and when mineral manures are added, the period of ripening is hastened, and its degree enhanced. A combination of mineral and ammonia salts, where the latter are not in excessive proportion, is beneficial to almost all crops, as to Cereals, Crucifers (turnips), Chenopods (beet, mangels), Solanums (potatoes), etc.

Minerals and Nitrate.—The produce in those cases where this combination is used is generally large, ripens early, is of a dark green color, with abundant foliage and relatively little stem. The per-centage of grasses has been large, that of Leguminosæ very small, and that of miscellaneous plants on the whole greatly reduced, effects which, in general terms, are very similar to those observed on the mineral and ammonia plots.

The mineral and nitrate appears to have encouraged the growth of *Poa trivialis, Bromus mollis,* and latterly of *Alopecurus pratensis,* while leguminous and miscellaneous plants have been discouraged. The following grasses are discouraged by nitrate : *Briza media, Cynosurus cristatus, Poa pratensis.* Leguminosæ in general and Umbelliferæ and some Composites are also discouraged.

Cerastium triviale, Plantago lanceolata, Galium verum, Centaurea nigra, and *Ranunculus,* are slightly favored by the nitrate.

The combination of minerals and ammonia favors the growth of *Poa pratensis, Agrostis vulgaris, Festuca ovina,* etc., more than does the admixture of mineral and nitrate. On the other hand, the following species, among others, are more benefited by mineral and nitrate than by mineral and ammonia : *Poa trivialis, Dactylis glomerata, Bromus mollis,* and *Lolium perenne,* etc.

In some seasons, especially in years of drouth, (1870), *Bromus mollis* was extremely prevalent, its deep roots giving it an advantage over others.

Effects of change of Manure.—The object sought at Rothamsted in changing the conditions of manuring has been to ascertain definitely to what particular ingredient in a mixed manure a particular effect is due, and to obtain confirmation of the results obtained by other methods. By adding or by withholding a particular salt, as the case may be, an answer to the question proposed may be obtained. In the following paragraphs the effects of the disuse of certain manures, and then of the substitution of one kind for another, will be very briefly alluded to.

Disuse of Manure of any Kind.—On a plot to which farm-yard manure was applied it was observed that while the produce was largely increased, more so indeed than under almost any other circumstances, the per-centage of grasses and of some of the miscellaneous weeds was increased, while the leguminous herbage was diminished. On discontinuing the dung the vegetation of the plot was observed gradually but uniformily to approximate to that of the unmanured plot, the number of species increasing without any marked preponderance of any, and good grasses like *Poa trivialis* giving place to poorer ones, such as *Festuca ovina*.

Disuse of Farm-yard Manure.—Another plot which originally received a combination of dung and ammonia, has been treated since 1864 with a small dose of ammonia salts only. Here the grasses and the Leguminosæ are diminishing as to numbers, but the luxuriance of those species that remain is increased. The miscellaneous weeds, especially *Rumex Acetosa*, and the Composites, are decreasing, *Ranunculaceæ* decline, and even more markedly so the *Umbelliferæ* and *Plantago lanceolata*, the latter plant being very sensitive to ammonia.

Disuse of Potash.—The first effect noticeable after the disuse of potash was a diminished produce of grasses. Leguminosæ have also continuously and strikingly decreased, while miscellaneous plants, especially *Achillea Millefolium* and *Rumex Acetosa,* have increased.

The increase of *Festuca ovina* is probably not so much due to any favoring effect of the manure as to the enfeeblement of its competitors. *Anthoxanthum odoratum* has increased, but almost all the other grasses have diminished. *Ranunculaceæ, Compositæ,* especially *Achillea,* have increased since the disuse of potash. Umbellifers, *Plantago lanceolata,* and *Rumex Acetosa* have decreased.

On the plot where ammonia is added to mineral manures, but where potash is omitted, the grasses show a large per-centage from the effect of the ammonia; the leguminous plants are almost banished, owing to the combination of unfavorable circumstances, *i. e.*, the presence of ammonia and the absence of potash. Ranunculaceæ are diminishing, as are also Umbelliferæ, Composites, *Plantago lanceolata,* and *Rumex Acetosa.*

As a general rule, it is recognized that the growth of plants is checked if the quantity of potash be reduced beyond a certain limit. Dehérain has recently shown that in the case of the buckwheat, starch is not generated from chlorophyll unless potash be present. If potash be added, then starch begins to be formed. Neither sodium nor lithium can usefully replace potash, though extremely little is known as to the functions of the latter. Salts of potash and magnesia have also a general tendency to augment the weight of leaves, while chloride of sodium favors the development of stem.

Substitution of Mixed Mineral Manures for Ammonia.—The consequences of the disuse of ammonia, and the employment in its stead of mineral manures, are shown in diminished produce, the grasses having been diminished, the leguminous and the miscellaneous plants increasing in number and proportion. *Festuca ovina* has been the most prominent grass, while *Lathyrus pratensis* has manifested considerable increase, and *Rumex Acetosa* has been the most prominent among the miscellaneous plants.

The greatest change after some years was, however, not in the distribution of the species, but rather in the character of their development and their increased tendency to form stem and seed.

Summary.—From the foregoing details it is manifest that the plants found on the several plots vary very greatly in number, in character, and in degree of development, according to the nature of the manurial agent employed, the ever varying character of the seasons, and the association or hostile competition of their neighbors. These several conditions rarely, if indeed ever, act singly, but almost always in combination. Circumstances are never exactly twice alike; a condition of absolute equilibrium is never attained. The nearest approach to it has been reached in the case of the unmanured plot on the one hand, and of the very highly manured plots on the other, but these, like the others, are influenced by climatal changes occurring now at one stage of growth, now at another. And even when a comparative state of equilibrium is attained, very slight causes, even such as may be roughly called accidental, as the injuries inflicted by insects, or parasitic fungi, suffice to disturb the balance and bring about a different arrangement and proportion of species, and a corresponding change in the development of individual plants.

As to the action of manures on the plants, it is comparatively rarely that they are employed in such quantities as to be absolutely destructive or poisonous. In most cases—even when a particular manure is proved to be more or less directly injurious to particular plants—the indirect harm accruing from the beneficial action of the substance on some other plant or plants, growing in association with them, is greater than the direct mischief. The manures act very differently on different plants, and vary in their action, even in the same species, according to the time and stage of growth at which they are employed. Some encourage the growth and development of their cellular tissues, at the expense of the woody and fibrous constituents, others favor the consolidation of the tissues, hasten the flowering period, and bring about an increased production of seed. But any change that may be induced is of a physiological kind, affecting the development of the individual, not the character of the species. By no combination of manurial elements is it possible to bring about that kind of change which a naturalist would consider specific.

CHAPTER VIII.

PRACTICAL INFERENCES.

Objects for which plants are cultivated, and the means of promoting them.—Plants cultivated for their roots—for their foliage—for their fibre—for their seeds.—Farming operations as aids to propitious climatal influences and as counteracting the evil effects of injurious ones.—Drainage.—Tillage.—Manures.—Change and variety of cropping.—Rotation.—Improvement of cultivated plants.—Selection.—Change of seed.—Cross breeding.

Having in the preceding chapters given an outline of the life-history of the plant, the machinery by which it is carried on, the manner in which that machinery fulfils its purpose, and the contest and competition in which living plants are always engaged, it may be well to indicate some of the points in which the history so outlined affects the practice of agriculture. Of course, were science perfect, which it is very far from being, and were practice uniformly intelligent and uninfluenced by mere routine or accidental circumstances, it would be found that no single detail of the plant's history was unimportant to the cultivator. As it is, owing to deficient knowledge on both sides, much of what the student learns in the laboratory has no application in the field, and much of what the farmer does on the land is without significance to the student.

It is the object of the series of Handbooks, of which this is one, to remedy this state of things, and to bring the two classes of workers more into accord, so as to ensure a greater amount of co-operation beneficial to both parties. The special value to the cultivator of scientific knowledge will probably be found in the power it gives him of availing himself of new resources and of adapting himself to altered conditions—no light matter in the present state of agriculture.

In endeavoring to turn to account some of the lessons which vegetable physiology is able to teach, we have in the first instance to consider what is the special object with which any particular crop is cultivated, because, as has been shown, the conditions suitable, say for the growth of wheat, are not those most fitting for the production of forage or of root-crops. Then it must be repeated that we grow plants for our own benefit, and only indirectly for the advantage of the plant itself. It may be that the objects for which we cultivate a particular plant are of such a nature as to be best compassed by means most favorable to the general health and welfare of the plant, as in the case of cereals, or it may be that we grow the plant for one particular product, to secure which we endeavor to promote disproportionate leaf-growth or root-growth, as the case may be, at the expense of the other organs of the plant, and so bring about what is really an unnatural and morbid condition.

In offering a few general considerations on these subjects, in addition to the numerous incidental references in other pages, it may here be convenient to arrange plants according as they are cultivated for their roots, inclusive of root-like organs, for their stems, and for their leaves, fruits, or seeds; omitting all those special details pertaining to what we may term the individual constitution of plants.

Plants Cultivated for their Roots, etc.—Under this head are included such crops as turnips, kohl rabi, potatoes, beet-root, mangels, and onions. In all of these the cellular tissue largely preponderates over the fibrous. The cells are filled with water and with various substances, such as starch and other secretions. In the economy of the plant these secretions are manufactured in one season, stored in the cells, and used up in the next season for the production of leaves, flowers, and seeds. The work of the leaves then of these plants differs to some extent according to season; those of the first year work to build up the plant and to store up the secretions in the "roots" or tubers, while the office of those produced in the succeeding year is more particularly to form and nourish the flower, fruit, and seed, and to secure the accumulation of nutritive matter in the seed. Unless the farmer requires the plants to seed, he uses up the roots for his own purposes before any demand is made upon the plant for flower and fruit building.

Speaking generally, the indications furnished by the nature of the plants, point to the necessity or desirability of a light, rich, friable soil for their culture, one which will permit of ready root range, and which, while supplying ample food, shall not harbor stagnant water. Rapid growth and vigorous leaf-action are also indicated, as, when these are secured, the cellular portions required grow in proportion faster and more freely than the fibrous portions, and the requisite secretions are stored the more readily in the roots. To ensure this rapid growth, more essential in an annual crop like potatoes than in those whose growth occupies part of two seasons, a warm aspect and a well drained soil are essential, while to ensure the formation of the secretions which render the plant valuable, free exposure to light is also requisite. Thus, hoeing and weeding owe their good effects not only to the removal of useless plants occupying space that might more profitably be employed, but they secure to the crop freedom from the shade of the weeds, and promote the access of light to the foliage and of air to the roots. The excessive action of the vegetative organs checks, to a varying extent, the development of the fruiting organs; indeed, the object of culture is to keep the plant growing and to prevent its flowering. If the seed of such plants is sown too early, growth is apt to be slow, and woody fibre is produced where succulent cells would be preferable, and, moreover, the tendency to produce flowers is enhanced by the high summer temperature which follows. If sown late, the growth of the vegetative organs is, for a time, rapid, because the soil is warmer and the sky lighter, while the tendency to form fibre and flower is checked.

The formation of subterranean tubers may be taken as an indication that the plant prefers a period of rest. The rest is, indeed, not absolute, but relative; and while little external change may be visible, it is probable, and in some cases certain, that considerable chemical changes go on during the period of apparent inaction. Under natural circumstances the rest is secured, either by the occurrence of heat and drouth, or of a very low temperature, the action of light being, in either case, excluded. These facts supply hints as to the proper mode of storing and pitting potatoes and roots. Moisture, light, and air should be excluded, the temperature kept as low as possible, short of frost, and what is of even more importance, kept as uniform as possible. By such means the roots may be kept dormant, and the waste to the farmer, which would occur from the unseasonable growth of the plant using up the food intended for his cattle or sheep, obviated.

Plants Cultivated for their Foliage.—Among these are the various green crops and forage plants, cabbages, mustard, clovers, sainfoin, lucerne, vetches and pasture grasses. Apart from the special requirements of each particular plant, such as the special influence of nitrogenous manures in promoting leaf-growth among grasses, and of mineral manures in fostering the leafy development of leguminous plants, and the special demands made by particular circumstances, the object, in all cases, is to ensure a rapid, abundant and nutritious leaf-growth. In some cases where otherwise too great acridity might be produced, it is desirable to secure shade to the leaves, and thus prevent the formation of the objectionable matters. Thus, in the case of cabbages the grower prefers those which "heart" well, *i. e.*, those in which the leaves are tightly packed one over the other, and do not readily separate ; and this tendency is increased by constantly selecting for seed those varieties in which this peculiarity is seen to be most marked. At other times the production of objectionable secretions is obviated by the process of "earthing up," as in the case of celery, or by tying up the leaves as in lettuces.

The development of leaves is of course largely dependent on the well-being of the roots, so that, in a general way, all those conditions of soil which are propitious to the development of roots are so also to that of leaves.

The requirements of particular plants are so varied, according to their affinity and the very diverse modifications of form and structure presented by their roots, that only generalities can here be alluded to. The cultivator must observe for himself whether the plants he wishes to grow are naturally shallow or deep-rooted; whether the roots break up into a dense leash of fine fibres encompassing and traversing in all directions the soil within a certain limited area; or whether, as in the case of lucerne, the "root" consists of a long, thick underground stem, capable of extending itself for many feet, and giving off, within a small extent, only a comparatively small number of fibres. The different forms of roots previously alluded to may be looked on as adaptations to different conditions of the soil, especially in relation to water, and the choice of site and mode of tillage must be governed by circumstances. Leaf-development is thus consequent on root-growth; but, in addition, an adequate supply of moisture and heat and full exposure to light are demanded. The adjustment of these agencies is rarely under the control of the farmer to anything like the same extent that it is in the case of the gardener. The gradener can often contrive, for instance, by appropriate modifications of treatment, to keep his plants in a growing condition, and to prevent them from "bolting" into flower, whereas the agriculturist is much more the slave of circumstances. Drouth and heat check his crops before their growth is complete, and induce premature development of fibre, of flower, or of seed. Excessive moisture and superfluity of rich food will cause the crops to become too rank in their growth, to develop immature succulent tissue, comparatively devoid of the nutritious secretions in which their value consists, and will check the development of flowers.

The observant eye of the farmer soon detects the unhealthy state of the crops by the color of the leaves. If, from any cause, root-action is deficient, or sun-heat and sunlight are lacking, the chlorophyll is not formed in sufficient amount, or is imperfectly developed, and the consequence is a yellow languid look about the leaves, betokening starvation. On the other hand, excessive size and succulence and too deep a green hue indicate an excess of stimulant nitrogenous food and a deficiency both of mineral food and carbon assimilation, in consequence of which growth is arrested. In such cases the amount of root-food taken up is out of proportion to the amount of leaf-food. If the season could be prolonged so as to ensure a longer duration of leaf-action, the balance might be adjusted, but this is rarely the case. Appearances in such cases are apt to be misleading to the inexperienced. There is an appearance of luxuriant vegetation with which the intrinsic nutritive value of the crop is not in accordance.

Plants grown for Fibre.—Apart from timber trees, hemp and flax are the only two crops generally grown on any large scale for their fibre, although the development of the straw of cereals is dependent on the same conditions. By hereditary transmission these plants manifest a tendency to produce fibre in greater proportionate amount than cellular tissue. Heat and light are specially requisite to ensure the formation and proper development of the fibre. Both are naturally plants of hotter, drier, more luminous climates than ours; nevertheless, if they can be grown rapidly they yield fibre, although the secretions of oil, in the seed of the flax (linseed), and of narcotic resin in the case of the hemp, are not produced in a relatively sunless atmosphere.

The formation of timber is, in general terms, the formation of fibre on a large scale. Root development, according to the special nature of the tree, of course conduces to the formation and proper development of leaves. Trees, from their root-range being wider than that possessed by herbaceous plants, can collect food over a larger area, and thus can extract nourishment from a comparatively poor soil which would starve other plants with less capacity for food collection and less duration of working life. The larger the leaf-surface, and the more fully and thoroughly it can be exposed to light, the greater quantity of timber and the sounder its quality. It may be requisite for certain purposes to have straight unbranched spars, and, in such cases, leaf-action is impeded and side-growth is arrested by thick plantations and neglect of thinning; but the actual amount of timber is necessarily less in such trees than in others of the same age allowed to develope freely on all sides. Coppice wood is also grown for a special purpose, which practically justifies that mutilation which, like most pruning operations, is of course at variance with natural growth. In the annual growth of timber it may readily be seen that the greatest activity of growth, *i.e.*, formation of new tissues, takes place in the first few weeks after vegetation commences. After that, the period of maturation or consolidation commences. A moist, warm, growing period is, therefore, most propitious. The process of maturation requires for its fulfilment greater heat, less moisture, and more intense light, and in proportion to the degree in which these requirements are satisfied, are the amount and quality of the timber. Should a wet, sunless autumn be succeeded by an early frost, when maturation is imperfect or incomplete, the results to the young growth, that is, to the crop of timber for the year, are correspondingly disastrous. The effect of mineral manures, especially potash, in promoting the development of the fibrous tissue in grasses, has been already alluded to; the largest absolute amount of straw being yielded by a mixed mineral manure with a large supply of ammonia.

Plants grown for their seed.—The remarks just made as to the development of timber as a consequence of maturation, apply *mutatis mutandis* to the development of the fruits and seeds. The farmer, however, especially requires for the culture of seed-plants which are grown as annuals, a rapid, uniform, vigorous growth, followed by a steady progress towards maturity, a condition favored by the gradual cessation or modification of leaf-work, and as simultaneous a ripening of all the fruits or seeds on the plant as possible. The mode of development of the inflorescence generally considered of mere technical or botanical interest, is here obviously a matter of practical importance, for plants in which the flowers and fruits ripen in succession are obviously less suited for the farmer's purposes than those in which the flowers of a particular inflorescence open approximately at the same time—as they do in the cereals. To ensure the production and good condition of the crop, as in the case of cereals, of beans, peas, buckwheat, etc., the first requisites to success are, of course, those which promote the proper germination of the seed, and then those which favor the due development of the root according to the nature of the plant. To a considerable extent the farmer is here master of the situation, and by drainage and tillage appropriate to the varied nature of the soil and the character of the season, he can promote and favor both germination and root-growth. Over leaf-action, independent of that which is the direct outcome of root-growth, he has less control, as he is at the mercy of the seasons. If cold, wet, growing periods are followed by dull, cloudy, maturing seasons, the crop must be deficient in quantity or quality, or both. The reasons for this deficiency have been repeatedly given. The farmer is not so able as the gardener to overcome these defects, but he is at least able in a measure to evade them by cultivating not only a variety of different crops, but numerous varieties of the same crop, some of which are sure to prove better adapted to sustain themselves under hostile conditions than others. Thus spring wheat, barley, or oats, may be made in a degree to supply the deficiencies of the autumn sown wheat, and tares, beans, peas, carrots, etc., etc., employed to compensate for the failure of other crops.

Manures.—By the judicious use of suitable manures at the right time, the farmer is also enabled in some degree to provide for and counteract the effects of unpropitious seasons. Farm-yard manure, for instance, not only increases the quantity of grain and of straw, but greatly improves the quality of the grain, as measured in pounds per bushel; and the same holds good of a mixed mineral and nitrogenous manure.

The time when nitrogenous manures can be most beneficially applied is a matter of great consequence, Messrs. Lawes and Gilbert having proved that the nitrogen carried off the land in the drainage water, is much greater when the manure is applied in the autumn than when used in spring. Another illustration of the use of manures of an opposite character to that just cited, is afforded by the use of common salt (sodium chloride) to check rank growth with its tendency to produce straw rather than grain.

The varying effects of season, according to the nature of the manure employed, suggest also that a variety of manures should be used. In the Rothamsted experiments, it has been shown that the seasons which proved most propitious to the unmanured crops, and to those to which only mineral manures were applied, were not equally so for the crops to which nitrogenous manures were applied; hence, says Sir J. B. Lawes, "the best season for land in low condition is not the best for land in high condition."

The varying effects of manure may be illustrated by a few figures taken from the Rothamsted "memoranda":

PRACTICAL INFERENCES. 119

thus, in the case of wheat, the average produce per acre over thirty years, was about thirteen bushels on the unmanured plots, as against thirty-six on highly manured plots (mineral and ammonia salts, and mineral and nitrate respectively), some plots also producing the largest quantities of straw, the nitrate producing rather more than the ammonia. The quality of the produce of wheat as measured in pounds per bushel is not so different, that on the unmanured plots being usually nearly equal to that of the highly manured plots. From this point of view, farm-yard manure proved more beneficial than the artificial nitrogenous and mineral manure yielding the largest quantity of grain. The corresponding figures in the case of barley, are seventeen and forty-nine ; the highest produce was with nitrate and. minerals, but the largest amount of straw was yielded with a manure containing a large proportion of nitrate of soda with minerals. Of hay, the average produce under like circumstances over twenty years, was two thousand three hundred and fifty two pounds on the unmanured, and six thousand nine hundred and forty-four pounds on highly manured plots (mineral and ammonia.)

In like manner, turnips varied from one or two tons per acre without manure to eight tons with superphosphate, and nine to twelve tons with superphosphate combined with nitrogenous manure, such as ammonia or rape-cake. Sugar beet produced, when unmanured, from seven to eight tons per acre in the earlier, to five tons in the later years, but eighteen tons with farm-yard manure ; nitrogenous manures increased the yield largely, but superphosphate was of no use to the beet and mangel. With mangel, the produce on the unmanured plot was from one to six tons per acre (average 4.6 tons), as compared with nineteen tons with farm-yard manure (or on the average fourteen tons). Potatoes varied from about half a ton on the unmanured, or about two tons on the average, to four to five tons with farm-yard manure, and to six to seven tons with mixed mineral and ammonia. The tendency to disease, however, increases with the higher manuring, in larger proportion than does the produce.

The data of science on the effect of manures must, however, only be taken as indications by the practical farmer, who must be guided by financial considerations and local conditions, in determining what it is best for him to do under particular circumstances at any given time.

An interesting circumstance may here be mentioned, viz: that many of our cultivated plants, such as cabbages and mangold wurzel, have sprung from wild plants growing by the sea, and are hence especially benefited by the use of salt as a manure. Onions, the growth of which is also favored by salt, probably originated from a wild stock growing in salt desert regions.

Fallow.—The good effects of this may be judged from the results of some Rothamsted experiments, in which the produce of wheat is recorded, after bare fallow, compared with that of wheat grown continuously on the same soil, without the intervention of fallow, and equally without manure. Under such circumstances, the average produce for twenty-five years after fallow has been eighteen bushels per acre, as contrasted with an average of twelve bushels where the wheat has been grown continuously. The weight per bushel was the same in both cases. The average quantity of straw after fallow was one thousand seven hundred and eighty-six pounds, as contrasted with one thousand two hundred and twenty-one pounds, where the crop was grown continuously.

Rotation.—The practice of rotation of crops is amply borne out by what occurs in nature and by chemical experiments, although not in the manner that might at first have been supposed. Leguminous plants, such as clover, beans, vetches, though containing so much nitrogen in their composition, are not only not specially benefited by nitrogenous manures, but they absolutely leave the land richer in nitrogen than it was before (Lawes and Gilbert), and thus prepare it for the growth of grain crops, which, though chiefly starch-producing, are yet specially benefited by nitrogenous manures.

In growing beans and wheat alternately at Rothamsted, it was found that eight crops of wheat grown alternately with beans supplied nearly as much produce (grain), and nearly as much nitrogen in that produce as were furnished by sixteen crops of wheat grown without manure. Here, then, the manure supplied to the beans not only favored those plants, but left a residue in an available form for the wheat.

Botanically, the good effects of rotation are dependent on the variations in the mode of growth and in the internal structure of roots, which allow of different layers of soil being utilized for plant-food, while the specially different requirements of different classes of plants obviate the exhaustion of any one ingredient, and give time for the accumulation of fresh supplies.

Improvement of Cultivated Plants.—This has already been alluded to, but its importance justifies repetition, the more so as to a considerable extent it is a matter that the farmer can do for himself. A series of small experimental plots might well be instituted on every farm. The first and perhaps most general use to which such trial grounds should be put, would be to test the quality of purchased seed, and ascertain what proportion might be expected to grow under different conditions. Other experiments should be devoted to the purpose of ascertaining what particular varieties are likely to do best in particular places. The investigator who sets to work to produce really improved varieties, has a more difficult task before him, owing to the number of excellent varieties already in existence. The consequence of this is that much labor and patience must be expended before any real improvement on what is already in existence can be expected, although there is the chance that a real advance may be made almost at once. The large capital employed by the seed-houses in raising and introducing improved varieties—real or so-called—is, at least, a testimony that the practice is pecuniarily profitable to the trader, and forms therefore a resource which the agriculturist might develop for himself to a larger extent than he does. He would reap the advantage on his own farm, even if he lacked the capital and enterprise requisite to conduct a commercial speculation away from it.

Selection.—The improvement of the races of cultivated plants, as previously alluded to, is indicated by Nature herself. In a wheat field or bean crop no two plants are exactly alike: one is more robust than another, one tillers more than the rest, the ears of one are plumper and fuller, this one grows earlier or later in spring, is therefore hardier or more tender, as the case may be. The careful observer notes these points, and instead of passing them over, endeavors to turn them to account by selecting the plant which shows a tendency to vary, taking seed from it and growing that seed another season. A certain proportion of the offspring is pretty sure to reproduce the desired qualities, probably even to manifest them in an enhanced degree. This leads to further and repeated selection, till, at length, a new race or variety is established. When it is remembered what vast results have accrued from the improvement of wheat and turnips by selection of this kind, it seems remarkable that further efforts are not made in this direction, and especially by selecting forms which observation would show are specially suited to a particular locality. Thus Rivett's red wheat produced at Rothamsted, on an average of eight years, fifty-three bushels of grain per acre, while Hallett's original red, grown under the same conditions, yielded only thirty-six bushels.

Change of Seed.—This is a practice followed with advantage by both gardener and farmer, for it is found that the crop is improved when seed even of the same variety is obtained from a distance where it has been grown under different conditions of soil and climate. In such cases it is better, where possible, to select seed grown on a poorer soil and under more unfavorable conditions than obtain where it is proposed to sow. The increased vigor and degree of fertility resulting from this process have been commented on by Darwin.

Cross Breeding by means of artificial fertilization is an operation not so much within the power of an ordinary agriculturist, owing to the delicacy of manipulation and length of time required to ensure results worth having. Such experiments would be better accomplished in the laboratory or experimental garden of the professed physiologist. The experiments carried out by Andrew Knight, Maund, and Sheriff, in the case of wheat and oats are, however, encouraging. When undertaken for practical purposes, it is specially desirable that mere haphazard crosses should not be encouraged, much less made purposely, but that a definite object should be pursued in a definite manner. The experimenter should set himself to work to endeavor to produce an earlier, a hardier, a more prolific variety, as the case may be, selecting for his purpose such varieties to breed from as he has ascertained by experience to be of such a nature as likely to yield promising results. It is not possible to give detailed instructions here as to the way in which cross-breeding may be carried out; it is difficult with cereals, less so with leguminous plants, easiest with the cabbage tribe. Indeed, as growers know to their cost, it is difficult to keep the races or strains of the cabbage-tribe pure and uncontaminated, owing to the facility with which the flowers are fertilized by insects which bring the pollen from the flower of some other variety. Too high breeding, however, often entails a delicacy of constitution or a defective productiveness which may be overcome by a fresh cross with a stronger strain.

CHAPTER IX.

DECAY AND DEATH.

Change, waste and repair.—Disturbance of the balance.—Death of the protoplasm.—Causes of death.—Natural death.—How plants die: impaired nutrition, starvation, suffocation, structural injury and paralysis.—Death beginning at the root.—Death beginning at the leaf.

Decay and Death.—Life is one continual series of changes—

"By ceaseless action all that is subsists."

The result of these changes is gain or loss, waste or repair, now one, now the other; or occasionally (and indeed generally) both simultaneously. While a proper balance and equitable adjustment between gain and loss exists, the plant lives and is healthy. Directly the balance is disturbed the plant may live indeed, but it becomes unhealthy; and if the disturbance continue—if waste overtake repair—if nutrition be persistently impaired, still more if it be arrested, the plant inevitably dies. This is that gradual and slow but sure march of destiny which comes sooner or later to all living things at their appointed time. That time comes when the tissues are—from that degeneration of their substance which may be a morbid process resulting from injury, or which may be merely the necessary result of the growth and maturation of the plant, or from the failure of supplies—no longer able to carry on their life-work. The period in question varies as to its occurrence. A wheat plant uses up its life within a few months, an oak tree within a few centuries, and there is every intermediate period.

But, in addition to changes which are the result of an inevitable march of events, death in plants sometimes comes suddenly from violence, life action is arrested in its full flow and tide, and by much the same essential causes as those which extinguish the life of animals. The death of plants is the death of the protoplasm. Prevent the access of oxygen to the living cell, and the movements of the protoplasm will be arrested and ultimately cease altogether. The properties and functions of protoplasm have already been explained. It is their destruction and their cessation which constitute death. But the death of a part is not necessarily the death of the whole, and the individual cells of plants are, as a rule, much more independent one of the other than are the individual cells of an animal. A root or a leaf, or a mass of roots, and a number of leaves may be injured, or even killed, and the plant will still live on, because there are more left behind uninjured; and these, relatively speaking, do not suffer from the damage done to their fellows. A tree may be stripped of its leaves and may still live, because there are cells which are uninjured, and which will do their parts towards compensating the injury. A felled tree by the roadside will often be seen pushing up new shoots in a manner that would be impossible in the case of an analogous injury done to one of the higher animals. The lower the organism, the less special in its conformation and construction, the more independent are its constituent cells. The higher the organism, and the more specialized its structure, the more dependent one upon another are the structural elements of which it is compounded.

Natural death may be described as an exhaustion of the protoplasm—its water evaporates or is drafted elsewhere; and so with its soluble or liquid contents—the insoluble and the useless remain behind. We see this in the case of the leaves every autumn; their protoplasm dries up, their chlorophyll degenerates and disappears; they are emptied of starch and other matters, which are conveyed to some other part of the tree to be stored up for future use by the new growths in the following season, until at length nothing is left but a framework of dry cellulose, a quantity of mineral or earthy matter, and such material as could not be dissolved or transported. In other organs the continuous maturing process at length results in the blocking up of the cells and tubes by continued deposit in the interior. Osmosis can no longer go on between them, for their altered structure prevents it, and in consequence the protoplasm disappears. Just as in human beings, the minute blood-vessels get "bony" or otherwise deteriorated in structure, so do the cells and fibres of plants become unfit to carry on the processes of life.

For the purposes of the cultivator, it is very desirable that he give an eye to the way in which plants die and to the causes in which induce death. The subject may be looked at from various points of view. From the structural point of view, death may begin in the cells of the root, in those of the stem, in those of the intermediate "collar," or in those of the leaves, and the appearances presented will be found to differ correspondingly.

From a physiological point of view death may result from starvation or from suffocation ; the process in each case may be partial and gradual or immediate and complete. Sudden death, or death by violence, results from the injuries inflicted by too high or too low a temperature, electric shocks, sunstroke, strong corrosives, and the like. These destroy life by disorganizing the protoplasm, breaking up the tissues, and arresting the natural movements, and cause death by destroying the machinery or paralyzing its action. The gradual effects produced by such injurious agencies as noxious vapors from kilns or factories, or as insects, or parasitic fungi are the same as those produced by starvation or suffocation. In the neighborhood of towns it may happen that the relative absence of oxygen, or, what comes to the same thing, the inability to use what there is, may conduce to the death of plants quite as much as the direct injury caused by noxious vapors. A perusal of the foregoing chapters as to the food and growth of plants will suffice to show why plants die ; and a consideration of their life-history as here set forth will show how the cause that may kill at one stage of active growth may be all but harmless at another stage of growth (see p. 64).

Death beginning at the Root.—When death begins at the root, the supply of water and of the air and food derived from the soil is cut off, and the plant ultimately perishes of starvation. Death at the root may result from injury inflicted by small parasitic worms, insects, rats, or other creatures—from unsuitable conditions of soil, too much or too little water, deficient drainage, deficient aëration, or from the presence of really poisonous ingredients. If the cause is widespread, so as to involve a majority or the whole of the roots, the consequences are proportionately serious ; if only a few are affected, the plant may not be visibly or materially injured,

The effects will be first and most especially obvious at the point of injury, and at the growing points, where the life-functions happen to be going on most vigorously at the time. Thus, if the young shoots and young leaves are in full activity at the time when root-mischief occurs, they will the soonest show the effect of cutting off supplies—they will wither and droop. If the process is slow and gradual, the leaves will become emptied of their contents, their chlorophyll will change color, the plant will assume a sickly yellow look very characteristic to the practiced eye. The older portions of the plant, with their reserve stores of water and food, may not immediately suffer; and it is from them that the materials requisite for any effort at repair and reorganization must, if it be possible, be made. Thus a plant may grow for some time after injury, and then suddenly flag because its reserve supplies are at length exhausted. It follows from this that death from starvation as a consequence of root-mischief is not generally a sudden, but more often a gradual process, the length of time of course varying according to the nature of the mischief, and specially according to the nature and condition of the plant.

Death beginning at the Leaf.—This may be appreciated from what has been before said as to the functions of the leaf. The leaf is an organ of nutrition, of respiration, and transpiration; if its functions are sufficiently interfered with, death will result, either from inanition or from suffocation, or from both combined. The power of resistance that a leaf has may be inferred from its structure. A thick, fleshy leaf, with layer after layer of chlorophyll-containing cells, with abundance of pores and a thick skin, is obviously better able to resist injurious agencies than a thin leaf whose delicate texture speedily withers and falls a prey to adverse circumstances.

DECAY AND DEATH.

The fall of the leaf in the case of deciduous trees has been already alluded to. It is only requisite here to say that, under the circumstances, ~~that~~ it is a natural process; and it is one that is provided for from the beginning. From a very early stage in the development of the leaf, a special layer of cells has been gradually forming at the base of the leaf-stalk at right angles to the others, which ultimately cuts off the dying and dead leaf-cells from the living tissues of the bark, much as the "drop scene" of a theatre separates the body of the house from the stage at the close of the performance. The leaf is emptied of its contents, and further supplies from below are eventually stopped off by the intervention of the layer of cells above described. A similar process takes place in the disarticulation of branches and of ripe fruits.

When disease or injury affects the leaves while still growing—as in the case of noxious vapors from chemical works or kilns, or in the case of insect injury—its effects are naturally most obvious and most severe at the growing points—the tips and margins of the leaf; and when the margins become thus arrested in their growth, while the disc remains in full activity, the result is a cup-shaped appearance or a crumpled surface resulting from the dead or dying portions having lost their elasticity and acting as a curb on the growing portions. Sun-burns and especially the attacks of insects and parasitic fungi are not so much confined to the margins, at least when the leaf is not in a growing state; they produce their effects in the shape of circular or irregular spots of brown decayed protoplasm. The effects of frost and the reason it kills have been explained in a former page. Nothing, however, can be advanced in explanation of the reasons why some plants of the same species, like the different varieties of wheat, are so much more tender than others. Death by the leaf is rarely immediately fatal, because there are many leaves, and they are not often all affected in the same way at the same time; and, moreover, in the case of plants other than "annuals," the fall and death of the leaves does not involve the death of the plant, as before explained. Even in the case of annuals, the life, like the nutritive matter, goes out of the leaves only to enter the seed.

Successor thus follows predecessor in one invariable rhythm, and although the limits of the individual existence can be but too readily recognized, the real end of life, so far as the whole race of living creatures—whether plant or animal—is concerned, is as incapable of being appreciated by the physiologist as is its beginning.

INDEX.

Absorption.. 10
   Amount of.. 14
   by leaves...................................... 29, 31
   by roots....................................... 23, 24
   of gases....................................... 29, 31
   of water.. 29
Alcohol.. 32
Ammonia Salts.. 17
   Action of... 102
   and mineral salts................................ 103
Annuals... 39
Anthers... 84
Bacillus.. 32
Bacteria.. 17, 26
Barley.. 19, 119
Bast-cells.. 27, 49
Beet... 20, 105, 119
Branches.. 39
Buds.. 39
Bud-formation... 82
Bulbs... 39
Bundles, woody.. 48
Cabbage.. 113
Cambium... 47, 48
Carbon.. 29
Carbonic acid... 29
Carnivorous plants.................................... 33
Caulicle.. 75
Cells, bast... 49
   growth of... 45
   their nature...................................... 12
   wood.. 49
Cereals..................................... 20, 87, 89, 105
Changes, chemical..................................... 88
   in plants..................................... 16, 130
Chlorophyll................................... 12, 28, 30
   degeneration of.............................. 114, 126
Circumnutation.. 52
Climbing plants....................................... 69
Clover.. 15
   Alsike.. 88
Color.. 115
Colza... 79
Contact, Action on leaves............................. 66
   roots... 59
   stems... 69
Cotyledons.. 74
Cross-breeding.................................... 85, 123
Death, at leaf....................................... 128
   at root.. 127
   from frost.. 64
   heat.. 65
   starvation....................................... 127
Decay.. 124
Deoxidation... 32
Diffusion... 11
   condition of...................................... 13
Drainage water....................................... 118
Embryo, formation of.............................. 74, 85
Endogens.. 48
Epidermis... 27
Exogens... 48
Eyes.. 40
Fallow... 120
Farm-yard manure................................ 106, 118
Feeding of plants...................................... 9
Ferments.. 17, 76
Fertilization... 83
   cross... 85, 123

Fertilization of cereals.............................. 87
Fibre crops.. 115
Flowers, structure of................................. 83
Foliage crops.. 113
Form of leaves.. 26
   as dependent on growth............................ 50
   of roots.. 22
   of stems.. 38
Frost, action of...................................... 64
Fruits, ripening of................................... 80
Gases, absorption of.................................. 29
   emission of................................... 29, 31
Geotropism.. 56
Germination.................................. 44, 48, 77
Germs... 17
Glucose....................................... 32, 76, 77
Grasses...................................... 20, 39, 91, 92
   cereal.................................. 20, 87, 105, 123
   pasture... 94
Gravitation, effects on roots......................... 56
   effects on stems.................................. 67
Growing points.. 46
Growth.. 44, 72
   of cells.. 45
   of leaves... 49
   of roots.. 47
   of stems.. 48
Hay.. 19, 88
Heat, action on leaves................................ 64
   on roots.. 87
   on stems.. 69
   (See also Temperature).
Heliotropism.. 62
Hops.. 69, 85
Hybridization... 88
Improvement of plants................................ 121
Inheritance... 73
Iron.. 18
Leaves.. 26
   absorption by..................................... 29
   action in darkness................................ 31
   of contact on..................................... 66
   of gravity on..................................... 62
   of heat on.. 64
   of, in light...................................... 30
   of light on....................................... 67
   of moisture on.................................... 64
   fall of.. 129
   feeding by.. 29
   forms of.. 26
   functions of...................................... 37
   growth of... 44
   movements of...................................... 55
   parts of.. 27
   sleep of.. 63
Leguminosae....................................... 93, 96
Light, action on leaves............................... 62
   roots... 57
   stems... 68
Ligule.. 27
Lime, action of.................................. 18, 101
Liquids, ascent of.................................... 42
   pressure.. 43
Malting... 77
Mangel... 105, 119
Manures.. 19, 118
   ammonia.. 102
   change of.................................... 105, 107
   disuse of.. 106

INDEX.

Manures, effects of... 20, 73, 100, 107, 108
  farm-yard... 106, 118
  mineral ... 100
    with ammonia ... 103
    nitrate ... 105
    nitrate of soda ... 102
    potash ... 18
    disuse of ... 106
    substitution of ... 107
    superphosphate ... 101
    with ammonia ... 103
Manuring, principles of ... 19
Maturation ... 78, 80
Meristem ... 47
Molecules ... 10
Movements ... 51, 56
  of leaves ... 55
  of protoplasm ... 51
  of seedlings ... 55
  of stems ... 53
  of the roots ... 52
NITRATES ... 17
  of soda ... 102
Nitrogen ... 17
  loss of ... 118
Nucleus ... 12
OBJECTS of cultivation ... 119
Onions ... 39, 120
Osmosis ... 10
Oxygen in soil ... 25
  Inhalation of ... 31
Ovule ... 84
PARASITES ... 33
Pasture plants ... 91
  grown without manure ... 98
Perennials ... 39
Perisperm ... 75
Petals ... 83
Petiole ... 27
Phosphorus ... 18
Pistil ... 84
Pith ... 49
Plants, carnivorous ... 33
  climbing ... 66
Plant food ... 16
Pollen, action of ... 84
  transport of ... 84
Potash salts ... 18, 20, 106
Potatoes ... 20, 39, 82, 121, 112, 119
Protoplasm, decay of ... 125
  its nature ... 12
  movement of ... 51
RADICLE ... 53, 60, 75
Reserve materials, transport of ... 75, 77
Ripening. *See* Maturation
Root ... 22, 24
  action of contact on ... 59
  gravity on ... 56
  light and heat on ... 57
  moisture on ... 58
  cap ... 22
  crops ... 111
  fibrils ... 24
  functions of ... 24
  growth of ... 47
  hairs ... 24
  movements of ... 52
  nature and origin of ... 23
  passage through soil ... 60

Root stock ... 38
Rothamsted, pasture at ... 91
  experiments 18, 19, 21, 35, 78, 109, 121
Rotation ... 90, 120
Runners ... 38
SALT ... 118
Salts ... 16
Sap ... 41
Seeds ... 116
  change of ... 123
Seed crops ... 116
Selection ... 73
  power of, by roots ... 20
Sensitiveness ... 56
Silica ... 15
Sodium, chloride ... 107, 118
Stamens ... 84
Starch ... 18, 31, 75, 77
Starvation ... 127
Stem ... 38
  action of contact on ... 69
  gravity on ... 67
  heat on ... 69
  light on ... 68
  moisture on ... 61
  growth of ... 48
  nature of ... 38
  uses of ... 41
  work of ... 38
Stigma ... 84
Stipules ... 27
Stomata ... 27
Straw ... 116, 118
Struggle for life ... 100
Style ... 84
Suffocation ... 27
Sugar ... 76
Sulphur ... 18
TEMPERATURE, effects of (*See* Heat)..
Tillering ... 40, 82
Timber ... 115
Transpiration ... 35
Transport ... 75
Tubers ... 39, 82, 112
Turgescence ... 45, 51
Turnips ... 102, 119
Twitch ... 38
VARIATION ... 73
Vegetation, alternate ... 121
  gregarious ... 90
Vessels ... 27
WATER ... 10
  absorption of ... 29
  diffusion of ... 11
  importance of ... 16
  ingress of ... 11
  supply of ... 10
  transpiration ... 35
Weeds ... 93, 97
  list of pasture ... 93
Wheat, composition of ... 15
  embryo ... 74
  laid ... 54
  pedigree ... 74
  produce of ... 119
  ripening ... 28
Wood ... 48
  cells ... 48
  structure of ... 48

www.ingramcontent.com/pod-product-compliance
Lightning Source LLC
Chambersburg PA
CBHW021937160426
43195CB00011B/1123